A Young Man After God's Own Heart

Jim George

HARVEST HOUSE PUBLISHERS
EUGENE, OREGON

Cover by Harvest House Publishers, Inc., Eugene, Oregon

Cover photos © svariophoto, Kuznetcov_Konstantin, melis / Shutterstock; lzf / iStock

A YOUNG MAN AFTER GOD'S OWN HEART
Copyright © 2005, 2015 by Jim George
Published by Harvest House Publishers
Eugene, Oregon 97402
www.harvesthousepublishers.com

ISBN 978-0-7369-5978-0 (pbk.)
ISBN 978-0-7369-5979-7 (eBook)

Printed in the United States of America

15 16 17 18 19 20 21 22 23 / VP-KBD / 10 9 8 7 6 5 4 3 2 1

Contents

A Personal Letter to You

Dear Friend,

As a guy, I love adventure...of every kind! And as you and I are about to begin a joint journey into adventure, I am thinking about one particular "extreme adventure." It fits our aim in this book of becoming a man after God's own heart.

I don't know how many times I've seen it from the air and admired it from the ground, but there's something very special about Diamond Head. That's the name of the extant volcano that forms a rugged, unmistakable landmark at the southern end of Waikiki Beach on the island of Oahu. On my last visit to this tropical island, I was challenged by my son-in-law (also an extreme adventurer) to not just look at Diamond Head, but to actually hike it!

So, off Paul and I went on an extreme adventure. We hiked. We climbed. We pushed on...until we made it to the top. And boy, was the effort worth it! The view across Oahu was incredible—truly an awesome sight.

Isn't that the way it is with the climb to experience the view from the top of any mountain peak, or high hill, or citadel where a castle or fort formerly stood—difficult, but worth it? But tragically, many young men never know what an utterly breathtaking view life is from the top (and I'm no longer talking about mountaintops!). Why? Because they never make it to the top of anything. Somewhere along their climb to "something," they stop, or get distracted, or stumble, or fall. And they never get back up, or they turn back, because the climb is too extreme.

But my new friend, that's not what I want for you. No, I want you to feel and experience that spectacular view from the top of your mountain called "life." And to help you get there, I have written this book. I originally wrote this book ten years ago. Now, ten years later, I'm thrilled to have another opportunity to add new insights after reading letters from and talking to young men from around the world who have benefitted from this book. I'm excited that the publisher has asked me to update the text and add two new chapters that reflect the feedback I've gotten from young men like you.

My desire as you read this book about your priorities as a young man is that you would not make some of the mistakes that I and others have made on the way to the top of our mountains. Mistakes can cost you many years in your quest for reaching the top—in your desire to make it, to succeed, to reach the summit, to become a man after God's own heart.

In this book my goal is to simply and clearly lay out some of God's priorities for you as you start your climb to greatness. Making these priorities your own is vital to preparing you for your life's climb.

To sharpen your focus and heighten the adventure, I have added some material at the end of each chapter. In "Tough Decisions for Today," you'll find a list of thought-provoking questions about the priorities discussed in that chapter. "The Cutting Edge" exercises are aimed at getting you into your Bible to reinforce your knowledge of God's priorities. You'll learn about the priorities you need to focus on, and you'll also learn some quick and easy ways to put them into practice.

So come on! The journey to understanding what God desires for you as *A Young Man After God's Own Heart* is an exciting one. Don't miss out on the quest…you will never be the same!

Your fellow traveler,

Jim George

Part One

Beginning the Adventure

1

What Is Your Heart's Desire?

I have found David son of Jesse,
a man after my own heart;
he will do everything I want him to do.

—ACTS 13:22

When I was 12 years old, my parents and I went on our one and only family vacation. Leaving from my boyhood home in Oklahoma, we passed through Dodge City, Kansas, on our way to Colorado. Of course, we had to stop in this historic old-west town and visit the famous Boot Hill Cemetery—you know, the place where all the famous outlaws are buried.

To this day I can still remember looking down at a tombstone with a message something like this:

Here lies Old Joe.
He died with his boots on.

And, would you believe it, at the end of the grave were two boots sticking up out of the earth! Later I learned that "Old Joe" wasn't actually buried there. And much later I found out that the words on a tombstone are called an *epitaph*, which means "a short tribute to a dead person."

Since that unforgettable visit to Boot Hill, I've collected a few other epitaphs. For instance, a Greek poet wrote this on the tomb of Spartan heroes in the fifth century B.C.:

Go, tell the Spartans, gentle passer-by,
That here, obedient to their law, we lie.

This next one was written in memory of the great English poet Shakespeare:

He was not of an age, but for all time.

Because I have a science degree from college, I like what was written about a scientist who died at the age of 85:

He Died *Learning*

All of these epitaphs were written by someone who knew the dead person. Benjamin Franklin, however, the famous American statesman, wrote his own tribute:

The body of B. Franklin,
Printer
Like the cover of an old book
Its contents torn out
And stript of its lettering and gilding
Lies here, food for worms.
But the work shall not be lost
For it will, as he believ'd, appear once more
In a new and more perfect edition
Corrected and amended
By the Author.[1]

There are also humorous epitaphs, such as…

> All dressed up and no place to go.

Or…

> Remember, friend, when passing by,
> As you are now, so once was I.
> As I am now, soon you will be,
> Prepare for death and follow me.

To which someone later added…

> To follow you I'm not content.
> Until I know which way you went.

To me, the epitaph that is the most inspiring of all is one found in the Bible. It's a tribute to King David, one of the most famous people in the Old Testament. Of him God writes,

> I have found David son of Jesse, a man after my own heart; he will do everything I want him to do (Acts 13:22).

Checking Out a Man After God's Own Heart

The life of David is a fascinating character study. David lived a life of extreme adventure. As a young man, probably about your age, he killed the giant Goliath. He once protected his father's sheep by killing a lion, and on another occasion, by killing a bear. His story is one of the great "rags to riches" accounts. David started out a shepherd boy…and ended up as a king. He became a great warrior and turned the tiny nation of Israel into a powerful kingdom that ruled most of the Middle East during the tenth century B.C.

But David's greatest claim to fame is God's epitaph, "I have found David…*a man after my own heart*."

I don't know about you, but I find this tribute curious. In it, God is stating His approval of David's heart and life. That is interesting because David's actions were not always godly! For instance…

- David was a warrior who "shed much blood" (1 Chronicles 22:8).

- David sinned with a woman named Bathsheba (2 Samuel 11:4) and then ordered her husband to be put into a dangerous battle position so he would be killed (2 Samuel 11:5-17).

- David had many wives (2 Samuel 3:1-5).

- David was a neglectful father, and his family suffered strife and tragedy as a result (2 Samuel 13:15-18,28-29; 18:33).

- David went against God's command and pridefully counted the number of his troops. The result? Seventy thousand of his people died in a plague (2 Samuel 24:10,15).

And yet God states, "I have found David…a man after my own heart." How can that be? How could God possibly praise a man with this kind of background?

Yes, David committed some sins that most of us can't even imagine or conceive of doing! Yet over the long haul, David wanted to be righteous. He loved God, and his heart's desire was to do God's will.

And do you know what? This is the kind of man God looks for today, too! God doesn't expect perfection. (We can sure see that from David's life!) However, in spite of all that David had done wrong in his life, God could still look at David's *heart* and say he was a man after His own heart—a man who desired to do God's will.

Checking Out Your Heart

This, my friend, is the grace of God. There can be no other explanation! By his actions, David didn't deserve God's blessings. But in his *heart*, David had the right desire. He longed to follow and please God, even though at times he stumbled and fell.

That brings me to an important question: Do *you* want to be a man after God's own heart? Or, put another way, is *your* heart's desire to follow after God?

You may think that's impossible. And if you do, you're not alone. If you're like me, you have a tendency to take three steps forward—then two steps back—in your spiritual walk with God. You may think that being a man after God's own heart is too high a goal. You may assume that it's not possible because of some of your past actions.

But you must never forget this: Where did God look? He looked at David's *heart*. And that's where God is going to look in your life, too!

That's where the adventure of becoming a man after God's own heart begins.

Checking Out God's Grace

My adventurous beginning in the Christian life was a little rocky. As a young man I went to church regularly...but that was it. There wasn't much depth to my faith. So when I went away to college, my heart desired many of the wrong things. I wanted a girlfriend, a neat car, plenty of money, lots of fun and friends, and I got them all...but then came my spiritual fall. I was a lot like the "lost son" in the story Jesus told in Luke 15, who...

> ...got together all he had, set off for a distant country and there squandered his wealth in wild living.... When he came to his senses, he said, "...I will set out and go back to my father and say to him: Father, I have sinned against heaven and against you. I am no longer worthy to be called your son" (verses 11-19).

Like this guy, I "came to my senses." I realized I was starving to death spiritually. I, too, looked up and came back to my heavenly Father. And, like the father in the story who was "filled with compassion" (verse 20), God graciously received me back. And life has been an extreme adventure ever since!

God, in His great grace, does this for any man—young or old—who comes to Him. And God does this for those (like me) who come to their senses and turn back to Him. From that point on, life is never the same. It's the ultimate adventure!

And now I've got a question for you. Have you drifted away from God? Do you ever feel like you are living in "a distant country" spiritually? Do you want to experience the powerful grace of God in your life? Well, if that is your desire, then read on!

Turning Your Life into an Extreme Adventure!

In the chapters to come, this section will ask the tough questions about your heart, your life, and the type of adventure you are on. So let's get serious here for a moment...and learn more about becoming a young man after God's own heart:

Question #1—When God looks at your life, what does He look for? Well, praise God, He doesn't look for perfection! Being a Christian is not about being perfect. In fact, the Bible says that there are no perfect men—no, not one (Romans 3:10)! Like David, and like me, every person—including you!—has sinned. Every person has disobeyed God. And it is that sin that separates us from God.

That's the bad news.

But now for the good news! The only perfect man who ever walked the face of the earth was Jesus Christ, God's only Son. He was truly a man after God's own heart. In every way and at all times, He did everything exactly as the Father wanted Him to. At Jesus' baptism, God said, "This is my Son, whom I love; with him I am well pleased" (Matthew 3:17).

Because Jesus was perfect and never sinned, He was able to die for your sins and mine. He paid the penalty for sin, which is death. The Bible tells us that "while we were still sinners, Christ died for us" (Romans 5:8). He was the perfect sacrifice for our sins. Because of what He did, we can be cleansed of sin.

Now, *that's* awesome!

Question #2—What does it mean to become a Christian? Briefly, becoming a Christian means...

- looking to God and His grace (Ephesians 2:8-9),

- repenting of our sins and turning away from them,

- accepting God's gift of eternal life through His Son's death for us,

- receiving God's mercy and forgiveness, and...

- living by His grace.

Now hear this: Being a Christian doesn't mean you won't sin anymore. You will still sin, just like I do. But sin will stop being the regular pattern of your life. Why? Because as a Christian, you are a new creature in Christ (2 Corinthians 5:17).

And what happens when you do sin? The Holy Spirit, who lives in you, convicts you so you can repent of your sin and return to enjoying fellowship with God (Psalm 51:12).

Question #3—What is your heart's desire? We've looked at David's heart and his desire to follow God. We've also looked at how God worked in my heart. But now for the most important question: What about *your* heart? What is your heart's desire? It would be great if, when God looks at your heart, He can say, "I have found you to be a man after My heart—a man who desires to do all My will"!

Question #4—Have you received Jesus as the Savior and Lord of your life? Perhaps you have already taken this step of faith and received Christ as your Savior. If not, or if you aren't sure, this is truly the First Step toward beginning the journey of becoming a man after God's own heart. A prayer like this can help you take this most important step toward turning your life into an extreme adventure:

> Jesus, I know I am a sinner, and I want to repent of my sins and turn and follow You. I believe that You died for my sins and rose again, that You conquered the power of sin and death. I want to accept You as my personal Savior. Come into my life, Lord Jesus, and help me follow and obey You from this day forward. Amen.

Now, my friend, if you are a new Christian as of this moment, write today's date here:_____.

Next, is there a Christian you know who would be really excited to hear about your decision? Give that person a call right now!

If you are or have just become a Christian, this one final epitaph—found on an actual tombstone in England—could be just for you.

> I have sinned;
> I have repented;
> I have trusted;
> I have loved;
> I rest;
> I shall rise;
> I shall reign.[2]

Tough Decisions for Today

What is your heart's desire? What do you desire most in life? And what do your actions show? Your hobbies, your friends, your music—do they say loudly that you desire to follow after God's own heart...or after your own heart? Jot down two or three changes you can make in your life.

Are you ready to turn your life into an extreme adventure—the adventure of following Jesus Christ? In light of what you've read in this chapter, list two or three qualities or steps you've learned are necessary to take when you follow Christ.

The Cutting Edge

Present yourself to God as one...
who correctly handles the word of truth.

—2 TIMOTHY 2:15

Read Luke 15:11-31. What does this story teach...

...about the father?

...about the son?

...about the older brother?

...about admitting your mistakes?

...about forgiveness?

What is God's message to your heart?

2

What Does It Take to Be All That You Want to Be?

As the deer pants for streams of water,
so my soul pants for you, my God.
My soul thirsts for God, for the living God.

—Psalm 42:1-2

One summer I traveled to Australia as a part of a team conducting leadership conferences for pastors. Australia is an incredible country. It is vast in size and the home of some of the strangest animals in the world—including kangaroos, koala bears, dingos, and wallabies.

The trip was one of those extreme adventures that don't come along very often! Our group was scheduled to conduct conferences in the four major cities. Plus we wanted to see the sites we had always heard about—the "outback" country and the Great Barrier Reef, to name a few. Because there was so much to do, this was going to be a fast-paced whirlwind of a trip indeed!

Our first conference was in Brisbane, Northern Australia—a truly awesome city! It basks in a pleasant semitropical climate. Palm trees line the streets, and pineapples grow in the fields along the roads leading to the country. And there are plenty of sandy beaches with terrific waves for surfing!

While staying in Brisbane, I heard a lot about the Great Barrier Reef. It is famous among divers and snorkelers the world over because of its crystal-clear blue waters. This famous reef extends some 1,260 miles along the northeast coast above Brisbane, and its width varies from 10 to 90 miles wide. This massive barrier was produced, strangely enough, by tiny sea creatures called *coral*. These little animals live and die in colonies which, over the centuries, have built this amazing reef, parts of which are hundreds of feet deep.

Now, the Great Barrier Reef doesn't look alive. But experts say that this astonishing reef *is* alive! In fact, it is growing even now as these tiny organisms live and die. Therefore, I accept and marvel over the fact that the reef is alive.

The Ultimate Power Source for Growth

In a similar way, the Bible is amazing, too! At first glance, it looks like any other book. The pages have black ink on white paper, like the newspaper or the TV guide. And yet there is something very different and very alive and powerful about the Bible. Why is the Bible unique?

Claim #1—The Bible claims to be the Word of God—"All Scripture is God-breathed"—which makes it the ultimate source for learning the ways of God—it "is useful for teaching, rebuking, correcting and training in righteousness" (2 Timothy 3:16).

Claim #2—The Bible claims to be true and never tries to justify its statements. You would assume that if the Bible is God's Word to us (Claim #1), we could also be assured of its truthfulness to us. That's what the psalmist concluded—"The law of the LORD is *perfect*" (Psalm 19:7). So, we can trust the Bible to give us correct advice for life and living.

Claim #3—The Bible claims to be alive. Consider this amazing statement: "The word of God is *alive* and *active*." How alive is it? "Sharper than any double-edged sword, it penetrates even to dividing soul and spirit, joints and marrow; it judges the thoughts and attitudes of the heart" (Hebrews 4:12).

The Manual for Real Men!

With claims like these, shouldn't you and I listen up and pay attention? Shouldn't we be at least a little curious about what the Bible has to say about life and our priorities?

No other book has the same effect on a person as the Bible! You can read books on any subject and receive information that will help you in one way or another. But when it comes to the heart and soul, only the Bible can bring true and lasting changes. I know that when I read the Bible, my life is transformed. I think differently. I act differently. I talk differently.

More importantly, if the Bible is God's own word—and if you and I want to live as men after God's own heart—then there's no better place for us to go for answers. Wouldn't you agree? God wrote the Bible to tell us about His love for us. And in it He shows us how we can enjoy a real and meaningful relationship with Him.

And I repeat—God wrote the Bible to let us know how we, as men, can best live our lives. In His Word He gives us His list of priorities that leads to successful and victorious living.

So…if your desire is to be a man after God's heart (and I believe you do or you wouldn't be reading this book, for sure!), then you'll want to learn what His plan for your life is. And you know what that means! You will need to take some time to read your Bible. It's God's Handbook for Real Men!

The Energizer of Growth

Have you ever thought about what your life would be like if you failed to grow physically into an adult man? Does that sound like your worst nightmare? It sure does to me! So like me, you would naturally consider this to be a serious tragedy. And equally tragic is a Christian young man who is not growing spiritually or whose spiritual growth has been stunted. You see, God expects you to grow spiritually as well as physically. In the Bible, growth is seen as a naturally occurring by-product of *life in Christ*. In fact, you are commanded to "grow in the grace and knowledge of our Lord and Savior Jesus Christ" (2 Peter 3:18). The writer of the book of Hebrews also assumed that with the passing of time his readers would grow to the point where they could be teaching others the basics of God's Word. But he had to rebuke his readers because they failed to grow: "Though by this time you ought to be teachers, you need someone to teach you the elementary truths of God's word all over again" (Hebrews 5:12). As I said, spiritual growth should occur naturally for those *in Christ*.

The Essential Element for Life

I love to run. In fact, I've been a runner since high school. Well, one bright sunny California Saturday, I decided I would see just how far I could run. So off I went running…five…ten…fifteen miles…. It was at the 15-mile mark that I figured it was time to head for home. One reason was because my running conditions were no longer very pleasant because the early morning sun had turned into the oppressive heat of midday.

Another reason was because I hadn't taken any water with me. I was beginning to crave water, the essential element for life. By the time I was within a few miles of home, all I could think about was water, water, more water, lots of water! My body ached for that life-giving substance. As I staggered into my house after 21 miles, I was truly panting for water.

The desire I had for water during that long-distance run is the kind of thirst we are to have for God's Word. Our physical body knows it cannot function without physical water. So, too, our spiritual life should realize it can't function without the "living water" of God's Word. The psalmist described this craving for God in this way:

> As the deer pants for streams of water, so my soul pants for you, my God. My soul thirsts for God, for the living God (Psalm 42:1-2).

Do you have this kind of craving for God and His Word? Just as water is the only substance that can relieve your thirst, God's Word is the only substance that can satisfy your spiritual thirst and ensure your spiritual growth. Only God's Word can give you strength in times of trial. And only God's Word can give you clear direction when you're trying to sift through the chaos of your busy life and juggle your schoolwork, family life, church activities, and any sports, music, or other special activities you might be involved in.

And here's good news! When it comes to spiritual growth, God does not leave you completely on your own. God's Spirit, who lives inside every believer, gives you the desire *and* the power to grow. Jesus promised that the Spirit will always be your Guide and your Helper (John 14:16-17,26).

So, with Christ, the Bible, and the Holy Spirit, God has given you all you need for spiritual growth. Now ask yourself—is the craving there? Why not satisfy it by spending more time with God in His Word?

As you read this book, I want your hunger and thirst for God to become more intense. I want your desire for His Word to turn your life into an extreme adventure of following after God's own heart. But the question is, Do *you* have those same desires?

The Choice Is Yours

I know you want to be all that God wants you to be. How do I know this? Because I don't believe you would still be reading this book if you didn't desire to please God with your life. I know, too, that you want to grow physically and to be as strong and athletic as possible. Every guy does!

And I also believe you want to be as *spiritually* strong and mature as you can be. So how can you move out in this direction? By starting with four choices. Each one of them is yours to make.

1. *Make a choice to meet with God*—God isn't going to make you spend time with Him. No, *you* get to make that decision! So you've got a serious choice to make if you want to meet with God.

   Think about this: How much time do you spend playing video games, watching TV, surfing the Internet, or hanging out with your friends? Why not take some of that time and choose to spend it with God?

2. *Make a choice to meet with God first thing each day*—You want to grow spiritually, right? Then do your spiritual push-ups and work out with God each morning. Read His Word—His Manual for Real Men. And pray—talk things over with your Commander-in-Chief.

My son-in-law is a Navy officer on a nuclear submarine. And there is hardly a day he doesn't have to get up by 4:30 AM. Getting up early is part of what men do. So don't you think you could start your day off with God by getting up just a *few* minutes earlier each day? It's good training for life, and it will make a difference in you.

3. *Make a choice to deny yourself for God*—The Christian life is one of willing sacrifice and commitment. It's like this: The whole world is saying, "Are you a Christian? Then prove it!"

   So what lesser-important activities would you willingly scale back or give up in order to gain something greater, to grow in your spiritual life? Would you be willing to…

   …say *no* to some time playing video games,

   …say *no* to some time watching TV,

   …say *no* to some time with friends,

   …say *no* to some time playing sports?

   Jesus said, "Whoever wants to be my disciple must *deny themselves* and take up their cross and *follow me*" (Matthew 16:24). Are you up for the challenge? If you are, I guarantee it will turn your life into an *extreme* adventure!

4. *Make a choice to say yes to the people of God*—One of the best choices you can make is to be around other Christians. Why would I say this? Because it's like

playing a sport or studying with someone who is more advanced than you are. *You* get better when you associate with those who have a passion for what they are doing, who are seriously committed to what they are doing.

And that's how it is when you are around other committed Christians. Their passion and commitment and zeal for God rubs off on you. It spurs you on! It challenges you, drives you, improves you, brings out the best in you. It helps make you all that you want to be.

So make the choices! Choose to…

…say *yes* to church attendance and the teaching you will receive there.

…say *yes* to your youth leaders when they ask who wants to meet one-on-one or in a small group.

…say *yes* to camps and retreats where you will get great teaching and focused direction from godly leaders (not to mention all the new friends you will make).

…say *yes* to every opportunity to be with other young people who are also committed to the things of God.

Turning Your Life into an Extreme Adventure

What's remarkable about spiritual growth is the way it impacts every area of your life. Not only will you be pleasing God and maturing as a Christian man, but you'll also have a significant and positive effect on those you come in contact with. Do you realize how many people you cross paths with each and every day? You have contact with hundreds of people—people whose lives you can positively influence if you are growing spiritually.

So are you up for it? Are you up for the adventure of an all-out effort for Christ? Are you ready to move forward on the path to spiritual growth…or to step it up a notch? And are you ready to see what will happen to you and all those you will meet along the way?

What is your heart saying? Are you listening to it, to God's message to you? Remember, God looks at the heart (1 Samuel 16:7). Here's a heart checklist to see if you are ready to embark on God's ultimate adventure for your life:

❏ *Do you want to be a strong, maturing man of God?* Then take care of first things first. Develop a closer relationship with God by praying, by reading His Word, and by obeying His commands.

❏ *Do you want to be a good son?* Then (again) spend time with God in His Word and in prayer, and He will give you everything you need and teach you everything you need to know about how to live out this major role of responsibility in your family.

❏ *Do you want to be a good friend?* Then cultivate a friendship with God. This contact with your Father and Friend in heaven will give you the wisdom to be a good friend to others *and* to make a positive impact on them.

❏ *Do you care about the spiritual life of your friends?* Then strengthen your relationship with God. That will allow the Spirit of God to work through you and help you to point others to Him.

❑ *Do you want your life to count?* Or asked another way: Do you want to be all that you can be? Then make God the Number One priority of your life. Put God first in each of your todays, and then all of your tomorrows will count in life and in eternity. All it takes is a desire to do God's will.

Do you have this kind of desire? As I said earlier, I'm one person who believes you do! I believe you are ready to tell God of your fresh commitment—or your renewed (or deepened) commitment to grow spiritually. I believe you are ready to begin that extreme journey that will ensure that your life does count.

Why don't you pause right now and talk to God? Thank Him for giving you the strength and desire to join Him on the fantastic journey ahead.

Tough Decisions for Today

Did you choose a time to be with God? What time? If not, begin your extreme adventure right this minute by making this important decision. Do it now. Then pick a place. What items do you need to set out on your journey with God?

Did you know that you can read through your Bible in one year if you will give it just 12 minutes a day? Will you give God 12 minutes today? Tomorrow? I have included an "Extreme Spiritual Workout Schedule" in the back of the book. Find today's date, read that portion of the Bible, and then check the box. How long did it take?

Is there an older guy or a youth leader at your church who can work with you one-on-one? Will you give him a call today? Like every Navy Seal, you need a "buddy" to team up with.

The Cutting Edge

Present yourself to God as one...
who correctly handles the word of truth.

—2 Timothy 2:15

Read Psalm 1:1-3. List all the actions and decisions made by a man who desires to grow spiritually. Then describe the spiritual health of a man who is following after God. Are there any changes you need to make today?

Read a similar description of spiritual health and growth in Jeremiah 17:7-8. What is spiritual health based on in verse 7? How is this person's condition described in verse 8?

What do these two passages teach you about your own spiritual health? About any changes you need to make?

3

What Can You Do to Make Your Goals a Reality?

Grow in the grace and knowledge of our Lord and Savior Jesus Christ.

—2 Peter 3:18

Eddie would go."

That's what the T-shirt said. *Who's Eddie?* I wondered as I thumbed through the T-shirt collection at the surf shop on Waikiki Beach. If you know anything about surfing, you know the name Eddie Aikau.

"Eddie was one of the greatest of the big-wave riders of the 1960s and '70s," answered a young sales clerk who looked like he had surfed a few waves himself.

"Where did that slogan come from?" was my next obvious question. The clerk hesitated a bit before answering.

"Eddie was a surfer who's become almost a myth. The stories say he was fearless in the water. He was so motivated to master 'the big ones'—the big waves—that even when others hesitated, 'Eddie would go.'"

"But Mister," my new surfing history teacher continued, "there was also another side to Eddie. His real greatness came in 1978 when Eddie was part of the crew of the Polynesian Voyaging Society's 'Journey of Rediscovery.' Their double-hulled replica canoe capsized in rough seas between islands in the Molokai Channel. The crew hung on all night and hoped for rescue, but by the next morning they realized they were being carried out to sea by the currents. Eddie insisted on going for help. His target was the island of Lanai, about 12 miles away. As he paddled off on a plank of wood, his last words were, 'Don't worry, I can do it. I will go.' Eddie Aikau was never found." Needless to say, after listening to this young surfer's story, I bought the T-shirt…and had a new hero!

If you ever travel to the island of Oahu, be sure and go to Waimea Bay Beach Park and see Eddie's memorial. And if you're really fortunate, you'll get to visit this spot in the winter and watch the famous invitation-only surfing contest held in his name. This event is for the select few who are motivated to brave "the big ones" on Oahu's world-famous North Shore Bonsai Pipeline.

Making Spiritual Growth a Goal

Edde Aikau's fame didn't just happen. Coming from a family with very few material goods, Eddie learned to surf on discarded plyboard. He bought his first surfboard at age 16 from money he had earned at the Dole pineapple cannery. He had a goal, and he was intent on fulfilling his dreams. And he made it happen.

The need for motivation—It's not hard to stir up the motivation to do the things that you really *want* to do, is it? I mean, you can make it happen whether it's surfing at Waikiki or "hanging ten" on the North Shore. If you're like most guys, you are always energetic and enthused when it comes to enjoying a personal hobby or hanging out with your friends or taking part in a sport. But when it comes to cleaning your room or going to school, doing your homework or maybe even reading your Bible, you probably find it hard to make it happen.

The things that motivate you—such as sports, fishing, hiking, swimming, surfing, or skateboarding, or whatever your favorite adventure is—can have a positive or negative effect on your life depending on how you handle them. For instance, as I shared earlier, I'm a runner. I love to run, and because of that love, I somehow manage to find the time to get out on the road and run. I do it because I really want to—and, like you, I end up doing what I want to do.

The need for balance—But we need to balance out what we *want* to do with what we *need* to do. The key is making sure we don't neglect the important elements in life as we pursue our education, interests, and fun.

Backtracking a little bit, you'll remember that in the last chapter we talked about the importance of turning your life into an extreme adventure of *spiritual* growth—an adventure that must start with your heart, with your desires and your goals. As a Christian, it should be natural for you to want to grow spiritually. It should be a burning desire. Like David, you ought to eagerly desire to follow God with a whole heart.

The need for goals—Coming back to this chapter, let's look one more time at your heart and your goals. What is the burning desire of your soul? My hope is that you're saying, "I want to grow in the grace and knowledge of my Lord and Savior Jesus Christ. I want to be a man after God's own heart. I want my life to have a positive spiritual impact on others…and on eternity. I want to be all God wants me to be. I want to make spiritual growth happen!"

Now, what can you do to make this goal a reality?

Making Spiritual Growth Happen

Spiritual growth is a terrific goal for you to have. For a Christian man it is extremely important, and it will most definitely have a positive impact on your life and on everyone around you. It's a priority goal! And yes, you also need goals that will prepare you for living in the world—goals that relate to your education and skills. (But let me quickly add that even though you need spiritual goals and educational goals, you can still have a little fun along the way. So don't sell your surfboard yet! Just make sure you keep your balance in life.)

What are the steps you can take toward making spiritual growth happen?

1. *Devote your life fully to Jesus Christ.* Have you already taken the step of receiving Jesus as the Savior and Lord of your life? As I said earlier, this is truly the first step to becoming a man after God's own heart. Once you become a Christian, the Holy Spirit comes into your life and works in you to fulfill God's will for you. You, like Jesus' disciples, are then ready to answer His call to "follow me" (Mark 1:17).

2. *Deal with sin.* Sin is any thought, word, or deed that goes against God's instructions in the Bible. And, my friend, you can take it from me—sin will always inhibit your spiritual growth. It sure stifled mine! Sin had a serious effect on King David's life, too. As you read about him in your Bible, you'll see how sin ruined this great man's career and his family.

   For example, consider David's sin with Bathsheba. To cover up the fact that he had gotten Bathsheba pregnant, David arranged to have her husband killed in battle (2 Samuel 11). For one full year afterward, David kept silent about his sins. Read David's personal description of what happened to him during that year:

> When I kept silent, my bones wasted away through my groaning all day long. For day and night your hand was heavy upon me; my strength was sapped as in the heat of summer. Then I acknowledged my sin to you and did not cover up my iniquity. I said, "I will confess my transgressions to the LORD." And you forgave the guilt of my sin (Psalm 32:3-5).

David experienced some very real physical side effects because of his unconfessed sins—his body wasted away, he groaned from pain, his energy and strength were sapped, his life was draining away. And the spiritual side effects must have been equally bad or even worse! David knew he had done wrong. And he knew he couldn't hide it from God.

What are you thinking?—"I'm sure glad that I'm not a major-league sinner like David. I haven't murdered anyone or gotten involved in sexual sin. My sins are just little ones. My sins aren't hurting anyone." Is this what you are saying to yourself?

Jesus put the seriousness of sin into perspective when He said that even if you merely get angry with someone, you have committed murder in your heart (Matthew 5:22). And even if you lust after a woman in your mind, you have sinned with her in your heart (Matthew 5:28).

So, the bottom line is, whether big or small, whether committed in public or in secret, whether acted out or hidden in your heart, sin is an insult to a holy God and must be confessed and forsaken. Friend, anytime you and I have unconfessed sin in our life, it hurts our relationship with God and our spiritual growth. Unconfessed sin also hurts our relationships with our family and our friends.

What will you do?—Be sure to take a few minutes to reflect on your own life. Is there unconfessed sin in your heart? Do you need to acknowledge your sin to God, as David did? As a man after God's own heart, David confessed his sin. He then experienced the wonderful cleansing and relief that results when we confess our wrongs and declared, "Blessed is he whose transgressions are forgiven, whose sins are covered" (Psalm 32:1).

If you want to experience the cleansing that comes with God's forgiveness and the freedom from the guilt that is caused by sin, then make it a habit to confess your sins to the Lord. As you do this, remember to thank God for His forgiveness. And when you've done this, you'll clear the way for you to move on to greater spiritual growth!

3. *Do away with spiritual laziness.* In years past, I was a part of a men's Saturday morning Bible study at my church. The study started at 7:00 AM, so I had to leave home at 6:30 to get there on time. Each Saturday as I drove to the church, my route took me by a golf course that was filled with men playing golf. Because many of the golfers

were already far along on the golf course, it was evident they had gotten there much earlier in the morning...like about 6:00 AM!

By contrast, when I arrived at church, only a few men were there to study God's Word. I was always amazed that so many non-Christian men were willing to get up so early on Saturday morning to play golf, but so few Christian men were willing to get up early to study and grow in God's Word.

Now, there's nothing wrong with playing golf or enjoying any other sport early on Saturday. My point (again) is that if you're failing to set aside some time for God in your life, and instead you are choosing to spend that time on your own pleasures and projects, then you're hurting your spiritual growth.

I know this isn't an easy matter. Even after years of being a Christian, I'm constantly having to evaluate my choices. Here are some questions that help me, and that you might want to ask yourself as well: Am I choosing the world over God and His Word? Am I choosing hobbies and sports to the point of excluding any time that could be spent reading my Bible and growing in faith? Am I choosing fun at the expense of being in a Bible study group?

Why not invite the Lord to help you with your choices, with your priorities? Why not determine to spend time with God in His Word and time with other guys who are studying His Word? Why not begin a spiritual "fitness program" and firm up your spiritual muscles? That's what being a man after God's own heart is all about.

4. *Decide the method of growth.* What's fantastic about starting a spiritual exercise regimen is that there are so many great tools available to help you grow. And, you can design your own regimen in order to accommodate your school schedule, responsibilities at home, and perhaps a part-time job.

You may want to start with resources that help you study the Bible by yourself. I have included some practical tips on how to study the Bible in the back of the book. You may also want to get involved in an exciting group Bible study program with other guys who desire to grow. Or, you can…

- listen to the Bible or the teaching of your favorite pastor or Bible teacher on CD

- watch a seminar on DVD

- memorize key Scripture verses

- create a personal growth plan that includes one or more of the above suggestions

Most important of all is that you read your Bible on a regular basis. God's Word will always be your main source of spiritual food. I once heard the startling statistic that less than five percent of all Christians ever read through their Bible even once! That means the simple practice of reading the Bible regularly will put you in the top percentage bracket of all Christians.

Friend, determining to read through your Bible is a decision you must make. Your youth pastor can't make that decision for you. Your parents or friends can't make it for you. No, *you* must decide! (To help make this happen, don't forget to use the "Extreme Spiritual Workout Schedule" in the back of this book.)

You'll definitely want to make a commitment to read the Bible daily, which will help you in your goal to grow spiritually. And while you're at it, ask someone else to read along with you. Hold each other accountable. You'll discover that sharing about your spiritual growth with a friend will be a great source of encouragement and support.

5. *Determine to be discipled.* If you want to grow, it's essential for you to be a learner. One of the best ways to learn is to find someone who can help lead you onward and upward toward spiritual maturity. That's what it means to be discipled or mentored in the things of Christ.

Every man who wants to be a man after God's own heart benefits from having a role model who provides counsel, guidance, and encouragement on a regular basis. When I was a young Christian, I knew I needed help. Did I ever! Quite frankly, I didn't have a clue about what I should be doing. So I looked for someone who was farther along in his spiritual growth to assist me in mine. I can only thank God that I didn't have far to go—there were several godly men in my church who agreed to come alongside me and help.

Over the years, I've met with many different men who have helped me to mature. I owe them a tremendous debt! And eventually I grew to the point where I could also start passing on to others what I had learned.

The Bible strongly encourages men like you and me to be involved in such discipleship. Paul exhorted one of his young disciples in this way: "The things you have heard me say in the presence of many witnesses entrust to reliable people who will also be qualified to teach others" (2 Timothy 2:2).

You've probably seen a relay race before. Well, that's what this verse brings to mind. Paul spoke these words to Timothy, his disciple, telling him to take the baton of God's truth and pass it on to other faithful men. These faithful men were then to pass that baton of truth on to others, who were then to pass it on to still others. This spiritual relay race has continued down through the centuries, and now the baton is being handed to you! Brother, you must take hold of that baton, run hard with it, and then make sure you pass it on to others. The Christian race, humanly speaking, depends on you passing on that baton faithfully and successfully. Let's not fail the Lord in our assignment!

6. *Dedicate your life to ongoing spiritual growth.* The Christian life and spiritual growth are not sprints. They are long-distance races that require lifelong perseverance. You grow in spiritual maturity as you run the race moment by moment, day after day, and year after year.

In many ways, running the spiritual race is a lot like physical running. If you stop exercising physically, your body may not show the results of inactivity for a while. But in time you will wake up and find that you can't run to the end of the block, and it's a short one at that!

In the same way, you may think you can get by without exercising spiritually, by not reading your Bible, or praying, or going to church. One day, however, you will wake up and find yourself spiritually flabby, out of shape, and wide open to sin...all because you didn't make a focused effort to keep growing day by day.

And remember, you can't rest on yesterday's growth. You must be dedicated to growing today... and every day.

Turning Your Life into an Extreme Adventure

As you consider the steps that make spiritual growth possible, you may be thinking, *This isn't at all easy!* It's true that growth doesn't just happen. Spiritual growth requires motivation and action on your part. But the benefits of such growth are phenomenal and well worth your effort. Here are some benefits you will experience when you focus your life on spiritual growth, on becoming a man after God's own heart. In addition to growing closer to God and showing Christlike behavior to a watching world, you will:

- possess the spiritual strength needed to defend yourself against temptation

- possess the spiritual resources needed to meet your everyday challenges

- possess the spiritual wisdom to make the right decisions about your future

- possess the spiritual maturity to choose the right kinds of friends and activities

We started this chapter by talking about motivation and goals. Eddie Aikau had both. His motivation and desire made him into a world-class surfer. Eddie's courage and skill have given us the slogan "Eddie would go." I hope Eddie's story has inspired and challenged you in your own personal life. It's good to have physical goals for your life now and for the future. You need them.

But as you see the benefits and blessings of growing physically, I pray that you are also motivated to set some spiritual goals for yourself. Life is made up of "the big ones"—the big waves, the big challenges, the big chances, the big decisions. Spiritual goals will give you all the skills and courage you need to endure and do battle when "the big ones" come. Are you ready for the challenges? I know you *can* do it. The question is, *will* you do it?

Eddie would go. Will you?

Eddie would do it. Will you?

Tough Decisions for Today

Read again the six steps for pursuing spiritual growth. What actions are you willing to take today in each of the following areas to ensure that you will grow spiritually?

1. *Devote your life fully to Jesus Christ.* What can you do today to be a living sacrifice (Romans 12:1-2)?

2. *Deal with sin.* Are there areas of unconfessed sin in your life that you need to acknowledge to God? When will you take care of it—when will you do business with God?

3. *Do away with spiritual laziness.* Write out a brief spiritual exercise program that you will begin this week.

4. *Decide the method of growth.* What study materials will you use? Have you started the Bible reading plan in the back of this book? If not, what are your plans for getting started?

5. *Determine to be discipled.* Who have you asked to disciple you? If you can't think of someone who can serve as your mentor, ask your youth leader to suggest someone.

6. *Dedicate your life to ongoing spiritual growth.* Write out a commitment to God about your desire to grow spiritually. Then date it. You may want to record this in your Bible. Refer back to this commitment often, and remember this day.

The Cutting Edge

Present yourself to God as one…
who correctly handles the word of truth.

—2 TIMOTHY 2:15

Read Hebrews 5:12-14. By the time this letter arrived, what did the writer expect of his readers?

What does "milk" indicate about the maturity level of the readers of this letter (verse 13)?

What does "solid food" indicate about the desired maturity of the readers (verse 14)?

What is a mature person able to do (verse 14)?

4

What Makes You a Man After God's Own Heart?

Part 1

Very early in the morning, while it was still dark,
Jesus got up, left the house and went off
to a solitary place, where he prayed.

—MARK 1:35

Before I became a pastor, I had a career in the pharmaceutical industry. Why pharmacy? Maybe it's because in my small hometown, the second job I held was in the local drugstore. (My first job was as a "carry-out boy" in the local grocery store.) In the pharmacy I swept the floor, stocked the shelves, and worked as a general "delivery boy." I liked the environment—it was clean, it was busy with people, and it was all about helping others get well. And my boss, a strong Christian, made the atmosphere a stimulating and pleasant place to be. I liked it so much that I began taking the course work that ultimately led to graduating from the University of Oklahoma School of Pharmacy.

Since finishing pharmacy school, I've worked as a pharmacist in drugstores and hospitals. Even after I entered the ministry, I continued on with the Medical Service Corps of the Army Reserves as a pharmacy officer. To maintain my pharmacy license, I'm required to know the characteristics, or marks, that are common for all medications in each classification of drugs. This makes it possible to know that certain drugs, when used, will obtain certain results. If drugs didn't have consistent characteristics or marks, we wouldn't be able to make reliable use of them.

A Heart that Obeys

Are you wondering what all this information about drugs and medications has to do with being a man after God's own heart? Well, just as classes of medicine have similar characteristics, so do men after God's own heart. In other words, every man after God's own heart will share some similar traits. And so far, we've considered the bottom-line mark of God's man. Did you catch it? Do you remember it?

A man after God's own heart is…
a man who yearns to please God,
a man who desires to grow spiritually,
a man who has a heart that obeys.

In our previous chapter we discovered that David was a man after God's own heart because he desired to do all God's will (Acts 13:22). This was true for David, and it's also true for any man, regardless of age, who desires to be a man after God's own heart. It's crucial that we know God's will…and obey it! While this is a rather simple way of defining all that's involved in true spiritual growth, it's the key to being God's man—knowing God's Word and obeying it. This characteristic or mark is ultimately the bottom-line mark of God's man.

Through the years, I've been blessed to have some men who belong to "the honorable class of men after God's own heart" as personal mentors. It was in these friendships that I discovered some additional marks of godliness. As I witnessed and observed the lives of these godly men "up close and personal," I began to realize that the marks of the godly men in the Bible are the same marks evident in all godly men. My friends and mentors possessed the same golden qualities as Bible heroes and men like Moses, Joseph, Nehemiah, Paul, and, of course, David.

What are some of the characteristics of a man after God's own heart? What qualities set such a man apart, whether it's a man like David, who lived 3,000 years ago, or a man—like you and me—living today? We've already seen in Acts 13:22 that such a man desires to obey God. Let's look at another primary mark here, and then we'll examine several more characteristics in the next chapter.

A Heart that Prays

When you read through the Bible, it becomes clear that the men who desired God were also men of prayer.

- *Abraham,* throughout his life, built altars and called upon the name of the Lord (Genesis 12:7-8):

  > The LORD appeared to Abram [Abraham] …So he built an altar there to the LORD.… From there he went on toward the hills east of Bethel.… There he built an altar to the LORD and called on the name of the LORD.

- *Moses* was constantly on his knees praying for God's direction as he led the nation of Israel (Exodus 34:8-9):

> Moses bowed to the ground at once and worshiped. "Lord…if I have found favor in your eyes, then let the Lord go with us."

- *David* prayed for forgiveness for his foolish decision to number the people under his rule (2 Samuel 24:10):

> I have sinned greatly in what I have done. Now, LORD, I beg you, take away the guilt of your servant. I have done a very foolish thing.

- *Solomon,* the great king of Israel, prayed for wisdom in order to judge the nation rightly (1 Kings 3:9):

> Give your servant a discerning heart to govern your people and to distinguish between right and wrong.

- *Daniel* prayed a prayer of confession for himself and on behalf of his people, asking God to return the Jews to their homeland (Daniel 9:2-19):

> I, Daniel, understood…that the desolation of Jerusalem would last seventy years. So I turned to the Lord God and pleaded with him in prayer and petition, in fasting, and in sackcloth and ashes. I prayed to the LORD my God (verses 2-4).

- *Nehemiah* prayed for God's protection while the wall of the city of Jerusalem was being rebuilt (Nehemiah 4:9):

> We prayed to our God and posted a guard day and night to meet this threat.

- *The apostles* prayed for guidance after the ascension of Jesus (Acts 1:14):

  > They all joined together constantly in prayer.

- *The apostle Paul* prayed constantly "for all the churches" where he had ministered (2 Corinthians 11:28). He was also in continuous prayer "night and day" as he constantly remembered the men he had discipled (2 Timothy 1:2-3). When he wrote to Timothy about how the church at Ephesus should worship, Paul urged "first of all, that petitions, prayers, intercession and thanksgiving be made" (1 Timothy 2:1).

  A bit later, Paul gave this exhortation: "I want the men everywhere to pray, lifting up holy hands" (verse 8). It's obvious Paul saw prayer as a primary ministry in his life, and he wanted all Christians to also be active in this important function of worship.

Mastering the Art of Praying

Do you already enjoy a meaningful prayer life? I hope so! But if you're like most Christians, there's probably room for improvement—maybe even *lots* of room! The biggest problem for me when it comes to praying is that it's easy to let other things crowd out most of my opportunities for prayer. Maybe you can identify with that problem, too. J. Oswald Sanders, a respected Bible teacher and author, put it this way:

> Mastering the art of prayer, like any other art, will take time, and the amount of time we allocate to it will be the true measure of our conception of its importance.[3]

So…what will it take for you and me to master the art of prayer, to develop a heart that prays?

Time—Obviously, *time* is a key element in developing a vital prayer life. If you and I want to be men after God's own heart, we need to set aside a time during the day to develop the art of praying and a heart for prayer. For me, the best time for prayer is early in the morning. I'm more likely to pray if I include it in my early morning quiet time along with my Bible reading.

On many occasions (and I know this probably won't sound very spiritual), I pray while I'm running. I take my prayer list in hand, or in my heart, and start running. As I begin pounding the pavement and praying, I seem to lose myself in prayer (and, as an added benefit, the pain of the jog is forgotten!).

For you, there may be other times of the day that are more appropriate for prayer. (But I bet early morning before school would be the best for you as well.) Whenever that time is, remember what J. Oswald Sanders said—the amount of time we give to something indicates its importance to us. So let's give prayer the time that it requires and deserves. After all, it's a mark—a vibrant mark—of a man after God's own heart.

Place—Next we need a *place* where we can talk with God. That place, like mine often is, might be out on a running trail or on a bike path, or the sidewalk as you're walking to school or to a friend's house or to some special activity. It might be in a quiet place at home before your family gets up, maybe your bed or desk. Or it might be some place at school during the lunch hour.

You don't have to be in a closet with your eyes closed to talk to God about the issues and desires of your life. All you have to do is make a choice. Rather than listen to the radio or a CD, or think about last night's ball game, you can focus on God and lift your prayers to Him. In a spirit of worship, you can recite and meditate on Scripture. And you can pray, talking to God about what's on your heart.

Jesus Christ is our perfect example of a man of prayer. Throughout the Gospels we see Jesus taking time to pray to the Father for strength and guidance for His life. In Mark 1:35 we read about the fact that He had both a *time* and a *place* for prayer:

> Very *early in the morning*, while it was still dark, Jesus got up, left the house and went off to a *solitary place*, where he prayed.

Pattern—We also need a *pattern* after which we can build a life of prayer. How did you learn to catch a ball, to ride a bicycle, to skateboard, or to do any other skill that's now a part of your life? You learned by *doing*.

So it is with prayer—we learn to pray by praying. There's no shortcut. The more regularly you pray, the more of a habit it becomes, and the more skilled you become. Then, over time, you'll gain a greater sensitivity as to how you can pray more effectively. Also, the more regularly you come to God in prayer, the more aware you'll become of His presence…and your sin. Repetition establishes a pattern, which helps you in becoming a man after God's own heart, a man who prays.

Lifestyle—Finally, the Bible calls us to a *lifestyle* or an attitude of constant prayer. We are commanded to "pray continually" (1 Thessalonians 5:17). And because we have the Spirit of God living in us, and because He knows what we should pray for (Romans 8:26-27), we can be purposefully praying at all times, in every place, by any pattern, as a lifestyle. Brother, a lifestyle of prayer is a distinct mark of a man after God's own heart!

I'm praying that our discussion about prayer is making you hunger to have this mark of godly character become more prominent in your life. That's what's been tugging on my own heart as I've been writing about it. (In fact, I'm resisting the urge to tie on my running shoes and hit the road so that I can spend some private time praying...because I want to try to finish this chapter first!)

Here are a few suggestions on how you can develop a more serious and consistent pattern of prayer in your life.

Yes, But How?

- *Start where you are*—For me, whenever I am out of the habit of praying, I start with just a few minutes each day.

- *Start with your priorities*—Pray for your own spiritual growth first. Then, pray for your family. Your parents and brothers and sisters need your prayers! So pray for each family member by name. Pray to be God's man in your home and in your family relationships. Next in priority order is your friends. Pray to be a strong witness to your friends. The list is getting long, so...

- *Start with a prayer list*—It can be as simple as a 3" x 5" card...or as comprehensive as a sectioned notebook. Write a list of the people and issues that are important to you and to God. Then pray faithfully for these people and issues. (What's great about using a card, even if you have a prayer notebook, is that you can tuck it into your pocket or school books or backpack and pull it out at any time or place, and pray down through your list of Very Important People and Issues.)

- *Start developing a pattern of praying*—Getting into the habit of praying means praying one day at a time. Prayer is a learned skill that anyone can develop. Start now developing the habit of prayer. All men after God's heart pray, and that includes you!

- *Start asking God for wisdom*—Ask Him to give you wisdom regarding how to pray (Romans 8:26-27).

- *Start reaping the blessings*—It's always thrilling when we see God answer our prayers. Lift your prayers to Him, and experience the blessings that come with answered prayer!

Turning Your Life into an Extreme Adventure

There it is, my praying friend. Do you want to follow hard after God, to be His man, to influence the lives of others for good, for eternity? Then prayer is a must. And the side effects are fantastic as you start reaping the blessings of answered prayer. As my friend and author, Terry Glaspey, remarks in his excellent book on prayer, "Prayer is, indeed, one of the most important factors in our spiritual growth. It can be said with absolute certainty that Christians who pray are Christians who experience spiritual growth."[4]

Dear brother, the list of the marks of a man after God's own heart go on...and so will we, in the next chapter. But before we move ahead, let's look again at what we've discovered so far about a man after God's own heart. He possesses...

- a heart that is saved,
- a heart for God's Word,
- a heart that obeys, and
- a heart that prays.

Take a few minutes to pray that yours is such a heart!

Tough Decisions for Today

Have you made the most important decision you need to make regarding prayer—that is, to start praying regularly? If not, what's stopping you? Be honest. Then list two or three steps you will take today to get going on the adventure into praying.

Make a prayer sheet or card for each member of your family. Then begin praying daily for them. Don't know what to pray? Then ask! Ask each family member what needs you can pray for, what the pressing issues of their lives are.

Begin a prayer sheet entitled "Decisions to Make." List your different decisions, big and small, and bring them to God in prayer each day. Ask God for wisdom and help. Then write down the answers as they come.

Pick out the person who gives you the hardest time in your life, and pray daily for that person. Do this faithfully for one month, and then write down how your thoughts and attitude about that person changed as a result of praying for him.

The Cutting Edge

Present yourself to God as one…
who correctly handles the word of truth.

—2 TIMOTHY 2:15

Read Matthew 7:7-8. What are Jesus' instructions regarding prayer? What does He promise as a result?

Read Mark 1:35. What do you learn about Jesus' prayer practices? In what way can you apply those same practices in your prayer life?

Read Philippians 4:6-7. How can prayer help when you have problems and issues?

Read James 5:16-18. What is the effect of the prayer of a righteous man—a man after God's own heart— according to verse 16? What is said about Elijah and his prayer life in verses 17-18? In what way is Elijah's prayer life a good example to us?

5

What Makes You a Man After God's Own Heart?

Part 2

God is spirit, and his worshipers must worship
in the Spirit and in truth.

—JOHN 4:24

What are the marks of a man after God's own heart? And how can you and I develop those awesome marks in our lives? As we get ready to discover more answers to that big question, I must warn you in advance: These characteristics are not easily attained. That's why they are not normally found in the average guy. No, these are *extreme* marks that set an exceptional man—young or old—apart from the crowd. But this is exactly the kind of unique man God is looking for:

—a man who will stand in the "gap" (Ezekiel 22:30),

—a man who "deals honestly and seeks the truth" (Jeremiah 5:1),

—a man who has "a good reputation with outsiders" (1 Timothy 3:7),

—a man who is "blameless" (Titus 1:6).

Do you desire to be one of these "few good men"? One of the marked few? One of a rare band of men who makes a difference in the world? Then let's go! We've already examined two marks of such a man: *a heart that obeys God* and *a heart that prays*. Now let's look at some other vitally important marks for the man who's committed to the extreme adventure of following after God.

A Heart that Praises

What usually comes to your mind when you think about David? If you're like me, you tend to think about David's "macho" achievements:

- He fought a lion and a bear.

- He felled a giant.

- He was a mighty man of war, conquering many foes.

- He was a great leader of men.

- He was a builder who launched the construction of "the city of David."

- He was feared by his enemies.

- He was one of the greatest kings of the ancient world.

There's no doubt David was a man's man, a leader's leader, and a warrior's warrior.

And yet David was a man with a tender heart toward God. David may not have always done what was right, but God was never far from his thoughts. He knew the "secret" of his success...

and it was God! On one occasion David came before the Lord in utter amazement, marveling at God's blessing, wondering, "Who am I, Sovereign LORD, and what is my family, that you have brought me this far?" (2 Samuel 7:18). David couldn't believe God's goodness, and he couldn't help but break forth in praise.

And there's more! As you read these additional words from David's heart of praise, think about how God has blessed you. You have been saved by a gracious God. You have the Spirit of God living in you to guide, direct, and protect you. I don't know anything about your family, but I would imagine that you have parents who love you and provide for your needs. So obviously you have much to praise God for. And even if a few things are "missing" in your life, praise God anyway. Your loving and all-knowing God knows who you are, where you are, and what you need. And He's promised to take care of you (Psalm 23:1). So…praise Him boldly and frequently! And David shows us how:

I will give thanks to the LORD…
I will sing the praises
of the name of the LORD Most High (Psalm 7:17).

Sing the praises of the LORD, you his faithful people;
praise his holy name (Psalm 30:4).

I will extol the LORD at all times;
his praise will always be on my lips (Psalm 34:1).

David sets a good example for us, doesn't he? He shows us that a real man after God's own heart is a man who is not afraid to express his love for God. Wherever David was, he worshiped his God through praise.

So you, too, as a man who loves God, should not hesitate in the least to praise Him. Whether you are walking with your friends, working on a project, doing schoolwork, or relaxing at home with your family, you as God's man should want to continually offer up praise to God (Hebrews 13:15).

Yes, But How?

How can you praise God more faithfully? Try these ways:

Meditate on God's power—I rarely go through a day without thinking about Paul's take on God's strength: "I can do all this through him who gives me strength" (Philippians 4:13). Do you have a problem today—a challenge you're facing, a problem at school that you must resolve, an issue at home or with a friend? Then help yourself to God's power! It's available to you, as promised through this one mighty truth. Remembering His power generates gratitude for God…which should result in praise.

Memorize psalms of praise—I love Psalm 118:24: "This is the day the LORD has made; we will rejoice and be glad in it" (NKJV). That's a real "attitude lifter," so to speak. As I square off with each new day and its challenges, this one verse that I've memorized helps to put a fresh spin on the day! Try it. Use it. And memorize it yourself. God's Word transforms each new day—no matter how difficult your tasks or your situation—into something praiseworthy.

Master God's promises—Estimates on the number of promises in the Bible vary from 7,487 to 30,000.[5] I urge you to pick one. *Any* one! I look to the promises of God zillions of times during each day to help me—promises such as this one: "Praise be to the Lord, to God our Savior, who daily bears our burdens" (Psalm 68:19). I find this promise encouraging to me when I'm burdened by a lot of work or by a book deadline. Perhaps you've found yourself burdened by schoolwork, friendship problems, or a busy schedule. Friend, help yourself to this promise and see what happens to your burdens. You'll experience freedom and renewed confidence and strength. And then you'll want to praise God like the psalmist did.

Marvel over God's provisions—Paul boldly declared, "My God will meet all your needs according to the riches of his glory in Christ Jesus" (Philippians 4:19). What a wonderful God you have—He promises to provide for all your needs! So you have even more reasons to praise Him.

Mull over the fact of God's presence—David never ceased to be amazed about the fact God was with him everywhere he went. He expressed his awe with these words: "Where can I go from your Spirit? Where can I flee from your presence?" (Psalm 139:7). Can't you almost sense exclamation marks after these thoughts? The answer to each of David's rhetorical questions is an obvious "Nowhere!" Think about it: It doesn't matter where you go—God is there. It doesn't matter what's happening along the way or when you get there—God is with you all the way.

Knowing that God is with you everywhere and all the time should make an extreme difference in your outlook on life. David's understanding of God's presence inspired him to declare, "I have set the LORD always before me. Because he is at my right hand, I will not be shaken" (Psalm 16:8). Now, that's confidence!

Magnify the Lord for His protection—King Saul, who sat on Israel's throne before David became king, repeatedly tried to kill

David. So, for much of his young adulthood, David had to be extra careful. Sometimes he even had to flee from town because of Saul's death threats. Yet in the midst of those life-threatening circumstances, David affirmed, "Even though I walk through the valley of the shadow of death, I will fear no evil; for You are with me" (Psalm 23:4). Whenever you are afraid, peace is yours when you remember that you are under God's protective hand.

Friend, as you remember the presence of God and praise Him for His power, His promises, His provision, and His protection, you will be strengthened and encouraged to face whatever life brings your way. So, just for today, put Psalm 34:1 into practice: "His praise will always be on my lips." It will revolutionize your attitude.

A Heart that Worships

David was a man of extreme passion, a true man after God's own heart. He loved God. He loved God's Word. He loved praying to God. And he loved praising God. And he had still another profound passion: going to "the house of the LORD." In fact, he longed to worship God. His heart cried out,

LORD, I love the house where you live (Psalm 26:8).

One thing I ask from the LORD, this only I seek:
that I may dwell in the house of the LORD
all the days of my life,
to gaze upon the beauty of the LORD
and to seek him in his temple (Psalm 27:4).

Friend, you, like David, should want to worship, to go to church, to be with God's people. It's a natural response for anyone who loves the Lord with all their heart, soul, mind, and strength (Luke 10:27). Weekly worship should be the highlight of all your activities throughout any week. You should look forward to the worship service at your church with anticipation. Think about it—when you go to church, you...

- hear God's Word taught and explained

- grow in your knowledge of the key truths of the Christian faith

- join together with others in corporate prayer

- worship God through music

- focus on others as you pray for those in need around the world

- interact with other believers

- leave the world for a few hours and participate in something that is 100 percent pure and good

- bond with others who belong to the Lord

- establish friendships based on a mutual love for the Lord Jesus

- study portions of God's Word for better understanding

- receive wisdom for the decisions you must make and any problems you face

- learn how to apply the Word of God to the everyday issues of your life

Man, oh man! Where else can you receive all of this...and more?!

And think about this: Your commitment to worship serves as an example to others. When you go to church, your commitment to Christ shows. It's right out there for everyone to see. Your friends and family witness your devotion to God. If your commitment to worshiping God with other believers is real, people will see it and be influenced by it.

Being a man of the Word, a man of prayer, and a man of praise and worship may not seem too exciting or too admirable, but God says it is. And now here's another mark of a man after God's own heart that may not seem to be very manly or very macho—a heart that serves.

A Heart that Serves

Possessing a heart that serves is another distinctive of the great men of God. There has never been a greater man than Jesus Christ. And guess what? He came to earth as a servant: "The Son of Man did not come to be served, but to serve, and to give his life as a ransom for many" (Matthew 20:28). And guess what else? You and I, as men who are following after the heart of God, are to follow in Jesus' footsteps (1 Peter 2:21), the footsteps of servanthood.

One day I met with a man with a heart to serve. He looked like he could have played linebacker for a pro football team. As we had lunch together, I noticed my new friend didn't eat much of his food. Instead, he talked on and on about how he loved to serve the people at his church. He was so enthusiastic that he gestured a lot as he spoke, and I almost got a little embarrassed because we were in a packed restaurant.

Nothing could keep this man's excitement down as he continued to tell me of his passion for serving God and His people. He constantly looked for opportunities throughout the week to serve the needs of fellow church members, and on Sunday he couldn't wait to get to church so he could continue his ministry of service.

This man's zeal for service may seem excessive or abnormal at first glance because of the "me" oriented society we live in. But his extreme desire to serve is Christlike. It's godly. As I said, it's another mark of a man after God's heart—a heart that yearns to serve.

As fleshly humans, our natural (and selfish) tendency is to take care of our own needs first. We like to make sure we have plenty of time for what *we* want to do. Then if we have any time or energy left over, we just might be willing to use it to serve someone else…maybe.

But as men after God's own heart, you and I need to make ourselves available as God's servants…like these men in the Bible:

- God spoke of Abraham as His servant (Genesis 26:24).

- Joshua was called "the servant of the LORD" at his death (Joshua 24:29).

- David, too, was called "my servant" by God (2 Samuel 7:5).

- Godly men were chosen by the church in Jerusalem to serve and help meet the needs of the widows (Acts 6:1-6).

- The apostle Paul referred to himself as a servant of God (Romans 1:1).

As you can see, service to God and His people is not an insignificant task. This is a mark of a man after God's own heart.

Turning Your Life into an Extreme Adventure

The slogan of the U.S. Marines is that they are looking for "A Few Good Men." Why a few? Maybe it's because they have learned from combat experience that a few "good men" are better that lots of "uncommitted men."

The Lord is looking for "a few good men" for Himself. But as we said at the beginning of the chapter, "good men" are hard to find. I hope that as you've read along, you have made the commitment to be one of God's "marked men"—one of His "few good men."

So with this commitment on your heart and in your mind, let's join together, as God's band of brothers, and make this prayer our commitment to be "marked men" for Jesus Christ— to be bold, to live bold, to stand out, speak out, and live out our loyalty to Christ:

Lord, I pray that as others look at my life, they would see the life of Jesus shining forth through me. Work in my life. Make me one of your "marked men." May others who see these marks want to follow You as well. I pray that I will...

...obey Your Word without question,
  ...pray without ceasing,
    ...praise You constantly,
      ...worship You continuously, and
        ...serve others unconditionally.

Tough Decisions for Today

How bold are you at offering up praise to God in public? Why or why not?

How can you turn up the heat on your commitment to your church? On your attitude toward church, the people there, and your service? What specific area of service can you commit to?

In the past, how have you viewed the role of a servant? Has this changed after learning about this mark of a man after God's own heart? Name one act of service that you can perform today to your family. To one of your friends. To an enemy.

The Cutting Edge

Present yourself to God as one...
who correctly handles the word of truth.

—2 TIMOTHY 2:15

Read Philippians 2:3-8. What is the theme of these verses?

Whose life is described in these verses?

What did He do? List at least three facts.

What changes will you make in your life—and heart—so that you can cultivate a servant's heart? List at least three.

How do these verses encourage you to worship and praise Jesus Christ?

What do verses 10 and 11 say about the worship and praise of Jesus Christ?

Read Acts 6:1-6. In a few words, describe the problem.

What was the solution?

What were the qualifications of the men to be selected—men who were men after God's own heart (verse 3)?

What is your attitude toward routine service?

How do Philippians 2:3-8 and Acts 6:1-6 help you to better understand your role as a servant?

Part Two

Getting on the Fast Track

6

Training at "Camp Home"
Part 1

Honor your father and mother.

—EPHESIANS 6:2

The month was February, and it had been raining for a full week. The earth was one big river of mud. And there I was, a private in the United States Army, experiencing boot camp at Fort Polk, Louisiana. My mission: Train to become a combat soldier. My platoon was in the second month of a four-month training cycle. We in the second platoon were going through just about every kind of physical stress that could be imagined. Up at 4 AM, our days consisted of a two-mile run before breakfast, hand-to-hand combat training, live-fire exercises, hours on the firing range, and push-ups beyond number—it was grueling!

This training was necessary if I wanted to be ready as a soldier. Without successfully completing this training, I wouldn't be prepared for the war that was being waged in southeast Asia at the time.

Now, you may not yet be ready for the type of training I received at Fort Polk, but you are most certainly ready for a different kind of basic life training. This type of training is a *must* for every young man preparing for the battles of life. And this training is received at God's official training outpost called "Camp Home," the place where you live. You as a young recruit must complete this training course in order to be prepared and experience victory in life's battles. You could sum it up this way:

> Your home is God's training ground for your future. Train well, and you will have the tools and will develop the skills for a productive and influential life. Fail in your training at Camp Home, and the possibility of a lifetime of failure is greatly magnified.

Sounds pretty extreme, doesn't it? Well, it is! Just as my combat training was extreme but necessary, so is your training at home. Basically the training consists of just one command, one order from God. And God doesn't grade on a curve when it comes to this command. It's either pass or fail: "Honor your father and mother" (Ephesians 6:2). That's it! Do this, and you pass the training curriculum for life at Camp Home. Do this, and you're on the fast track for becoming God's man.

Honoring Your Parents

This command in Ephesians 6:2 was not a new concept that the apostle Paul came up with on his own. It was first given by God to Moses way back in the Old Testament, way back in Exodus chapter 20. Have you ever heard of the Ten Commandments? Well, honoring your parents is commandment #5.

The first four commandments give instructions about your relationship with God: have no other gods, make no idols, don't misuse the name of God, and remember the Sabbath day and keep it holy (Exodus 20:1-11).

The next six commandments deal with your human relationships. And do you know what the first one is?

If you said, "Honor your father and mother" (verse 12), you're right. That's God's first "order" to you, which means this commandment is extremely important! It is not a suggestion. It's a command, and you as a young man after God's own heart are to honor your parents.

Now, what does it mean to honor your parents? Here's a definition I like because it doesn't leave any wiggle room. No loopholes, "what ifs," "yes, buts," or "later, dudes."

> What does it mean to "honor" parents? Partly, "honoring" means speaking well of them and politely to them. It also means acting in a way that shows them courtesy and respect (but we are not to follow them in acts of disobedience to God). Parents have a special place in God's sight. Even those who find it difficult to get along with their parents are still commanded to honor them.[6]

Did you catch the part of the quote that says, "Parents have a special place in God's sight"? What do you think that means? We could say it means God is on your parents' side when it comes to your training. It's a tough job that your parents are asked to do. You think you have it tough? All you have to do is *obey*. But here's what your parents are asked to do:

- Parents are commanded by God to teach their children (Deuteronomy 6:7).

- Parents are commanded by God to train their children (Ephesians 6:4).

- Parents are commanded by God to discipline and correct their children (Hebrews 12:7).

And just as you are accountable to God for following His command to obey and respect your parents, your parents are accountable to God for following through on His commands to them. So don't be too hard on your parents. They have a big challenge from God for your training. When things get a little tense around your house and you wish you could trade your parents for different ones, remember that your parents are only trying to do their job.

Dishonoring Parents

Whenever I think of honoring and obeying one's parents, I can't help but think of several examples of men in the Bible who didn't show respect to their parents. They dishonored their parents. Or, put another way, they were men who were not men after God's own heart:

Esau was the son of Isaac and twin brother of Jacob (Genesis 25:19-26). He didn't honor his parents by asking their blessing on his desire to marry. He didn't ask, and therefore his marriage was a source of grief to his parents (Genesis 26:35).

The two sons of Eli, the high priest of Israel, were disobedient and evil. And because Eli didn't discipline them, God judged both Eli and his two sons. The sons died in battle, and Eli died when he heard the news of their deaths (1 Samuel 2:12-36).

These are but a few examples of men who didn't honor their parents and brought heartache and pain to themselves and their families. But God says it doesn't have to be that way. He added a promise to His command that we should honor our parents. He promised that when you respect your father and mother, it will "go well with you and…you may enjoy long life on the earth" (Ephesians 6:3). Because Esau was disobedient, things didn't go well around the house. And the disobedience from the two sons of Eli led to their deaths.

Checking Out God's Word

Do you want things to go well around your house? And do you want a better life? Then look at these verses that were written by God especially for you as a child. Are you ready for some *extreme obedience?*

> My son, do not forget my teaching, but keep my commands in your heart, for they will prolong your life many years and bring you prosperity (Proverbs 3:1-2).

> Children, obey your parents in the Lord, for this is right. "Honor your father and mother"—which is the first commandment with a promise—"that it may go well with you and that you may enjoy long life on the earth" (Ephesians 6:13).

> Children, obey your parents in everything, for this pleases the Lord (Colossians 3:20).

Yes, But How?

Are you convinced yet about the importance of honoring and obeying your parents? God's Word is clear on this matter. Now the question is, How can you show this obedience and honor to your parents?

Are you ready for some answers? Then start where you are right now, and ask God to give you the courage and stamina to see this training through, not just until you graduate from "boot camp" at home, but for your entire life. Master the upcoming areas of your life, and you will stand tall and take your place on the front lines of life. You will be able to go into life's battles knowing that God is on your side. Doing these *little* things today will equip you to do the *big* things tomorrow and in life.

Your attitude—Honoring your parents all starts with you. No one can make you honor and obey them. Oh, they can try. They can physically discipline you. They can ground you forever. They can do all sorts of creative things to make you obey. And they may succeed in getting a positive response from you... at least on the outside. "Yeah, yeah, I'll clean up my room. Yeah, yeah, I'll do this or that," you mutter. "Anything to get you off my back!" But on the inside, in your heart, you are defiantly saying, "I may be agreeing on the outside, but on the inside, no one's gonna tell me what to do!"

Well, I hope I'm not talking about you! Maybe I'm talking about the guy who lives down the street, or the rebel dude at school. No, as a man after God's own heart, you are to desire to honor and obey your parents. Sure, you may slip back into some old habits once in a while. And sure, at times it's difficult to obey. But it's important for you to understand that Camp Home is the training ground for life...and the first lesson God wants you to learn there is obedience and respect toward your parents.

Why? Because it's pretty much a proven fact: If you can't or won't obey your parents at home, then guess what? You can't or won't obey others, either! Whether they are your teachers, your coaches, your church leaders, your future bosses, and ultimately God, you won't respect and honor them, and you won't be God's man.

Obedience is a discipline that is learned at home. You will never be a man after God's own heart without cultivating an attitude of obedience—an attitude practiced and perfected at home.

Your room—"Oh, no, not my room! That's my only area of privacy!" you say. Well, I'm not talking about making your room open to the public. What I am talking about is keeping your room neat and picked up. God created the earth and brought order out of chaos. But most guys I know are trying to reverse God's law of order and turn order into chaos in their rooms.

However, a man after God's heart makes every effort to turn things around, to follow after God's design for order, to do things God's way. You should make it a point to always leave things better than they were when you found them…and that includes your room. Keeping your room clean and orderly is a habit that will take you far in life.

All because you learned a simple discipline at home…in your room, when you picked up your dirty socks, on your own, without having to be prompted by your mom's threats…you'll find yourself being much more organized at school, in your work, in everything you do. Keeping your room clean may seem a small discipline, but it's a habit that will make a big difference in every area of your life.

Turning Your Life into an
Extreme Adventure

Because the training you are receiving at Camp Home is so important, let's pause for a moment and think about what we've learned before we continue on with more training elements in the next chapter.

You may have heard it said that *attitude is everything*. And especially a biblical attitude toward obedience. I know that when life gets tough or things go wrong, keeping a right attitude becomes more difficult. But just because something is difficult doesn't mean it's impossible.

With God's help, you *can* change your attitude. Paul shows you the kind of attitude you should want to have: "Have the same mindset as Christ Jesus...he humbled himself by becoming obedient to death" (Philippians 2:5,8). Ask God, the Father, to give you the same humble attitude Jesus had—an attitude of willing obedience.

Tough Decisions for Today

Read again the definition of what it means to honor your parents (see page 81). What one thing can you do today to show honor and respect to your parents? Write it here. Then write out how you are going to follow through and do it.

What is the one thing you can do right now to care for your room? What have you been putting off, neglecting, or willfully refusing to do? Honor your parents—and God—by doing it now.

How would you describe your attitude at home? How would your parents describe your attitude? How would your brothers and sisters describe it? Do you need an attitude adjustment? What specific changes will you make? Ask God for the strength to follow through. In one week, ask yourself these same questions again and check your progress.

The Cutting Edge

Present yourself to God as one…
who correctly handles the word of truth.

—2 TIMOTHY 2:15

Read Hebrews 12:1-3. What was Jesus asked to do? What was His attitude as He faced the cross? What should your attitude be as you fulfill God's will for your life, especially obeying your parents?

Read Psalm 40:8. What attitude did the writer have toward God and His will? Do you consider yourself to "delight" in and "desire" to do God's will or to "dislike" it? Are there any changes you ought to make?

Read Luke 2:41-52. Describe this family scene. Who are the people? What are the places? What happened? In the end, how did Jesus honor His parents?

7

Training at "Camp Home"

Part 2

Join with me in suffering,
like a good soldier of Christ Jesus.

—2 TIMOTHY 2:3-4

Fast forward with me in my military career. It's not February in Louisiana. It's August...in the middle of the Mojave Desert. And it's not raining. In fact, it hasn't rained in two years. We are 50 miles from nowhere, at the Desert Warfare Training Center, where most of the U.S. Army's desert training takes place.

Dawn is just breaking. The temperature is already 85 degrees, and it's only 6 AM. Later in the day the heat will reach 115 degrees...in the shade! I am a U.S. Army Reserve officer in charge of a medical aid station. My team's job is to treat the various injuries of those working around tanks, armored vehicles, and under extreme heat conditions. (Oh, did I fail to mention the snakes, scorpions, and sand fleas?)

My men and I are "in the field," where I had just spent the night on a stretcher in the back of one of our ambulances. No, I wasn't hurt. It was simply the best place to sleep! Early in the morning, I was suddenly awakened by a slight rumbling noise.

As I rolled off the stretcher, the noise and the shaking of the ambulance increased noticeably. I had slept in my fatigues, so it was easy for me to quickly make my way to the top of the ridge above us. Off in the distance, I can see a great cloud of dust.

I know exactly what it is. I also know that soon the sound will be so deafening and the shaking of the earth so severe that I will hardly be able to stand because of the hundreds of Abram M1 fighting tanks rumbling toward us from the desert. These hundreds of tanks and men had been training for war.

Little did I or anyone else know that some months later, many of these same men and their tanks would be in the deserts of the Middle East battling Saddam Hussein in the Persian Gulf War.

Continuing the Training

In the previous chapter, we began to talk about training—training for battle. And the battle is not for a piece of land, but for a heart—your heart. We've been discussing the disciplines that will prepare you for the battleground of life—for a life that will honor God and serve others.

The starting point of this training is to honor and submit to your parents. We have already considered a few of the lifelong benefits of developing and sustaining a positive attitude toward your parents as they do their part to prepare you for your future. And remember, a key element of this positive attitude is submission.

Why is a submissive attitude important? Consider my son-in-law Paul, who joined the U.S. Navy and was commissioned as an ensign. But then came OCS (Officer Candidate School). The Navy shipped Paul off to boot camp, where he arrived the first night just in time for "chow" (that's military talk for dinner). Each new recruit walked into the "mess hall" (another military term) and guess what awaited each one? A mess tray piled high with nothing but peas!

At that moment Paul had a decision to make. Would he obey orders and eat the peas (which he hated) or not? I'm sure many thoughts were flowing through Paul's mind right about then. But because he had been trained to obey at home, it was easy to obey the drill sergeant at OCS and chow down the wretched, pale green, overcooked peas. Today Paul is a Commander in the submarine corps and waiting for his orders to command his own nuclear submarine. He was trusted with becoming an officer because he proved his trustworthiness through obedience.

I've already mentioned how important obedience is in your relationships with other people. But I haven't yet mentioned the effect that "following orders" has on your relationship with God. And this is really crucial! It's been said that "a child has to learn obedience in the home or he will never learn obedience to the Heavenly Father."[7] It really is true that respecting and obeying your parents prepares you to be obedient to your ultimate authority, God.

With this fact fresh before us, let's look at a few more of the little yet important things you can do to train yourself and your heart at Camp Home. And keep in mind, it's these little things that will propel you onto the fast track for getting ahead in life…and possibly open the door for you to command your own nuclear sub or fly a jet off an aircraft carrier!

Your cooperation—Have you ever played team sports? You probably have, even if it was tag football on the front lawn, round-robin volleyball at the beach, or pickup basketball in the park. In order for your team to do well, what must happen? Every team member must cooperate, right?

Well, it's the same way with you and your family. God wants you to function as a team member with the rest of your family and to live in unity and harmony (Psalm 133:1). He wants you to glorify Him as you honor and obey your parents (1 Corinthians 10:31).

Your parents probably want the entire family to function as a team as well. And your job assignment from God is to cooperate. Yes, at times it will be difficult for you. There will be times when you can't see any reason for the demands your parents are making. But a young man after God's own heart will go ahead—with a positive and pleasant attitude—and obey his parents.

Here's the way it works: If your parents want you and your family to go to church, you go. If they want you to go back to church at night, you go. If they need you to watch your little sister or brother while they run an errand, you do it. If they need help around the house, you give it. If they want you to watch less TV, you watch less TV. Whatever is needed or requested from you by your family, you give it. Why? Because a man after God's heart cooperates. He's a team player. He helps the team be a winner before God and before a watching world.

And the benefit? You will learn how to be a team player for all the times you need to be one in the future—in your jobs, marriage, family, church, you name it—even if it means eating peas!

Your honesty—Do you want to stay on God's good side? Then don't lie. God says that He hates seven things, and one of them is "a lying tongue" (Proverbs 6:17). Telling lies is hurtful, dishonest, and wrong.

Truthfulness starts at home. Learn to be honest with your parents. Honesty is important even in the small things of life. Let's say you are asked a simple question by your parents. The consequences of lying in your answer are minor, but still, there are consequences. Now you have a decision to make: You can tell a "little white lie," or you can tell the truth. Each time you lie or tell the truth, you are forming either a bad and sinful habit, or a good and godly habit. If you learn to lie at home, eventually you will find it all too easy to lie to your friends, to your teachers at school, to your youth pastor, to your future boss…and to God.

So don't get used to lying. Start telling the truth at home. Be honest with your parents and your brothers and sisters, and you will be honest with others, too—including God.

Your prayers—I don't know what it is about us guys, but we don't communicate very much. Girls love to talk. They talk to each other, their parents, their teachers, to anyone who will listen, including God. It seems that when it's time to pray at youth group, usually the girls are the ones who volunteer to do the praying.

Well, even if we as guys don't communicate much with others, we still need to develop our skills at communicating with God. That's not only because prayer changes things, but because prayer also changes us and our hearts. Do you love your parents and your brothers and sisters? I know you do. Then one of the greatest acts of love you can give them is to pray for them. So why not show your love for them? Pray for them!

Think about it for a moment. Who's praying for your parents? Who's praying for your dad who works long hours to provide for you and the rest of your family? And how about your mom? Who's praying for all her roles and responsibilities? Maybe your grandparents are faithful to pray for your family. But it's very possible that if you're not praying for your family, no one is! So pray for them. If they are stressed out or going through a hard time (and they probably are), pray for them. You can never pray too much for your parents and family members.

And don't forget to pray for yourself, too. Pray for your attitude. Pray for an obedient heart. Pray for wisdom to say and do the right things at home, at school, and at church. Growing up sometimes feels like a lonely journey. But with Jesus as your Friend and Guide, you are never alone. Talk to your Friend, Jesus. He is always there to listen and to steer you on the journey.

Your money—Your money management is another area where Camp Home can be a valuable help. When I was growing up, my parents taught me two habits that have stayed with me up to this day.

First, my mother taught me how to *give money* to God. (It's all His in the first place, you know. He's only asking us to be stewards of His money and take good care of it.) Each Saturday my mother and I would sit down and place our giving money into a church offering envelope. Then at church on Sunday, together we would place our envelopes in the offering plate as it was passed by. Today it's very easy and natural for me to give money to God and God's work. Why? Because this was how I was trained at home.

How about you? Are you training yourself to give God a portion of your earnings, whether the money is from doing chores, working a part-time job, or even from your allowance? God will be honored, and you will be blessed when you give.

Then my dad taught me how to *save money*. Each week he took me to the local bank and stood with me while I deposited my meager earnings into my savings account. Saving, like giving, became an ingrained habit that has never left me.

My friend, obviously there's a lot more to wise money management. But if you learn these two basics—how to give to God and to save your money—you will be well down the road to handling God's money well, as a faithful steward. So start your financial training today, right in your home.

Your service—Who do you think was the greatest leader who ever lived? Most people would probably name some famous general or a great statesman. But I'm sure you, like me, would accurately name Jesus Christ as the greatest leader who ever lived… and still lives today.

Why? Not only because He is the Savior of all who put their faith in Him, but also because He inspired—and is still inspiring—young and old, men and women, black and white, rich and poor, to follow Him. Do you remember what we learned earlier in Matthew 20:26-28? Do you recall what Jesus said was the most important characteristic of anyone who wants to be a great leader? A quality that Jesus Himself possessed and liberally demonstrated throughout His life?

The answer is *a servant's heart*. Jesus said be a servant, and you will be great. And where better can you be trained as a servant than in your own home? At every opportunity, ask your parents and your brothers and sisters the four little words of a servant—"How can I help?" Develop the sincere habit of using these four words at home, and one day you will be great—you will be a great servant-leader. And you will be a man after God's own heart.

Here's what one leader of a large church writes about being a servant—about the humility that it fosters and the strength that results:

> If you want to be great according to Jesus Christ, be a servant. Humility shifts our focus outward, on others and off of ourselves. Humility calls us to serve God, our ultimate CEO, by serving others…. Humility will enhance your leadership at every level.[8]

And friend, it all begins at Camp Home.

Turning Your Life into an Extreme Adventure

How's your combat training going so far? Camp Home is a little tough, isn't it? Well, I'm sure you know what the coach always says: "When the going gets tough, the tough get going." And besides, no one said it would be easy. In fact, Jesus said, "In this world you will have trouble" (John 16:33).

Preparing to turn your life into an extreme adventure by living for God, whether at home or away from home, is a challenging task. But it's one that must be mastered if you are going to be successful in life, if you are going to be a man after God's own heart. God has provided the perfect place in Camp Home for you to get the basic training you need.

Consider yourself as one of God's "special forces" soldiers, as being on assignment from God. And major on following this advice that the apostle Paul gave to another young soldier: "Join with me in suffering, like a good soldier of Christ Jesus"

(2 Timothy 2:3). I urge you...be willing to pay the price that is required of you at your home:

- Obey your parents.

- Follow their leadership.

- Learn from their wisdom.

- Seek their advice.

By developing your character at Camp Home, you will grow into exhibiting the kind of conduct in life that honors God... and your parents.

Tough Decisions for Today

Can you relate to my son-in-law's decision regarding the peas given to him in the mess hall? What request from your parents are you resisting? Or what tough decision are you facing today? What is keeping you from "following orders"?

How would you rate your cooperation with:

Your parents?	Poor	Fair	Good
Your brothers and sisters?	Poor	Fair	Good
Your friends?	Poor	Fair	Good
Your school?	Poor	Fair	Good

What can you do to improve in the area of cooperation?

What is your attitude toward money? What steps are you taking to be a better steward of your money?

What would you do if you found a wallet on the sidewalk as you were walking home from school (and no one was around...and there was money in the wallet!)? Or put another way, how do you rate in the important area of honesty? What improvements can you make?

The Cutting Edge

Present yourself to God as one...
who correctly handles the word of truth.

—2 Timothy 2:15

Read Proverbs 6:17-18, and notice the seven things God hates.

What does He say about lying?

What does He say about cooperation?

Read again James 5:16-18. What is required in order for your prayers to be effective?

Who was given as an example of a righteous man?

What was the outcome of his prayers in...

verse 16?

verse 17?

What do these verses from James teach you about your own prayer life?

8

Going Somewhere That Counts

Jesus grew in wisdom and stature,
and in favor with God and man.

—LUKE 2:52

I didn't have a chance! I grew up in a small town in Oklahoma where most of the men worked at the local factory. A high school education was all that most boys wanted or needed to get a job there. Education for most of us just wasn't considered to be that cool. *But never mind,* we thought, *there was always the factory in town!* There were always plenty of jobs to go around, right?

Wrong! The factory closed right after my senior year.

So then, what's a guy to do? If you had been like many of my friends, who had relied on the factory and thought a high school education was enough to get a job, you had a real big problem. Sad to say, that was the situation for many of my buddies who hadn't taken school seriously because they counted on getting a job at the factory.

Fortunately for me, Mr. Walker came to my rescue during my sophomore year. I was working at the local supermarket bagging groceries. I was enjoying the job and had even won several "bagging contests." However, Mr. Walker, one of the local pharmacists, approached me at church one Sunday and offered me a job at his pharmacy. I had just received my driver's license, and Mr.

Walker wanted me to work as a delivery boy (and do some other chores around the store). What a deal—I could drive the delivery truck all over town, and let someone else pay for the gas! And I would get a 15-cent-per-hour raise, to boot!

Sharpening Your Focus

Have you ever heard the saying, "Aim at nothing and you will hit it every time"? Well, that's what happened to many of my buddies from high school. And I was going down the same road… until Mr. Walker came along. He started working with me and giving me direction for my life. He got involved in putting me on a more certain track to success. And soon, he got me interested in pharmacy work.

Suddenly, I had a direction—a focus. I knew where I was going. I wanted to be a pharmacist. That meant I would need to go to college…which meant I would have to do well in high school…which meant…. I think you can see where I'm going with all of this, right?

We all have a choice: We can either drift along through life, hoping the factory (or the gas station, or the repair shop, or whatever) won't close, or we can focus on our future, do our best at school, and actively prepare for our journey into the future. It takes effort to make something of yourself in life. And it's even better if you don't wait for a Mr. Walker to come along. Start preparing now…by focusing yourself, setting goals, and working hard. Then, whatever God brings your way…and whenever He brings it…you will be prepared for the adventure.

Here are just a few verses from God's Word that focus on listening, learning, and growing. Follow God's advice, and you'll get on the fast track to an extreme adventure that leads straight into His plan for your life.

Let the wise listen and
add to their learning,
and let the discerning get guidance (Proverbs 1:5).

My son, do not forget my teaching,
but keep my commands in your heart,
for they will prolong your life many years
and bring you peace and prosperity (Proverbs 3:1-2).

For the LORD gives wisdom,
and from his mouth come knowledge
and understanding (Proverbs 2:6).

Grow in the grace
and knowledge of our Lord
and Savior Jesus Christ (2 Peter 3:18).

Yes, But How?

Recently I was on the U.S. Navy base near my home. While I was there a sailor walked by wearing a T-shirt with these words:

Extreme Navy
Rough seas, high winds,
flight decks pitching...
You can't just do it,
you've gotta take it
to the extreme!

Friend, when it comes to going somewhere that counts, you will never get there without preparation. If you want to succeed, then you must take some extreme measures (at least they are extreme by today's standards!). You're going to have to try to do well in school. Whether it's junior high school, high school, technical school, or college, an extreme adventure takes training. So, how are you going to pull this training thing off?

First, you must *acknowledge* God's plan…and start thinking about your responsibility to Him. (I know we guys don't always like hearing this, but we need to.) If you are a Christian, God is calling you to fulfill your obligations and responsibilities at home, at school, and at work. You can't skip over any part of life that's unpleasant and expect to be successful. For example, a successful sailor has to go through boot camp first.

Just think about Jesus. He was God in a human body. He lived out His human existence in a normal fashion. He "grew in wisdom and stature" (Luke 2:52). Nothing was left out of His life or upbringing…including the process of learning. Because He didn't skip out on the essentials, He was able to fulfill His purpose for coming to this earth.

God the Father had a plan for Jesus' life. And that plan included the normal process of developing physically, mentally, and practically. And guess what? God also has a plan for your life, a plan you need to follow. This normal course includes physical activity and bodily development. It also involves home life, family relationships, and (you guessed it!) learning to work around the house. And it demands schooling and the work training that will enable you to grow in wisdom, knowledge, and personal discipline.

My encouragement to you is that you accept the work required for you to grow to intellectual maturity. Acknowledge God's personal plan for growth in your life right now. (He, for sure, more than anyone else, wants you to go somewhere that counts!) And shoot up a "Thank You" prayer to Him for His plan for your future.

Second, you must *welcome* God's plan. You should thank God that He *has* a plan for you! Think about it—the God of the universe has a plan...specially designed for you! Now that's truly incredible!

So, own the fact that you have an amazing future waiting for you around every corner. Sure, you don't know what God has planned for you, but you ought to get excited about preparing for it and anticipating it. And it doesn't matter what kind of work you go into—every kind of job requires that you gear up for it. Every profession is demanding, and therefore requires focused preparation now.

Third, you must *excel* in God's plan. The Bible says, "Whatever you do, work at it with all your heart, as working for the Lord, not for human masters" (Colossians 3:23). That "work," for you as a young man on the rise, includes your schoolwork. You need to develop the study habits necessary for doing well in school. You need to work hard. And you need to develop life skills.

And here's another "need": As ridiculous as it may sound, you need to keep reading, or learn to read better. Amazingly, research studies tell us that many adult men haven't read a book since high school! If you want to dominate in the extreme adventure called "learning," then you must develop and maintain your reading skills. You'll never excel in any area if you don't read. As the saying goes, "A reader is a leader, and a leader is a reader." Going back to the sailor's T-Shirt—

> You can't just do it,
> you've gotta take it to the extreme!

Do you agree that mental discipline is necessarily in order for you to gain the information you need for living a life of wisdom and adventure? You will notice I didn't say academic excellence gives you wisdom. No, your hard work at school gives you knowledge—knowledge that's important. But note this too—knowledge is not the goal of your education. There are many educated fools in this world! No, instead of mere *knowledge*, your goal is to get *wisdom* (Proverbs 4:5,7). Wisdom is *the proper application* of knowledge and information. That's what you want…and need!

Finally, you must *model* God's plan to others. Going somewhere that counts takes extreme measures! Sometimes we don't like to stand out, but if you are taking things to the extreme, then here are some questions you will want to ask yourself: If someone were to watch me at school…

- would they say I am different?

- in what ways would they say I'm different?

- would they see why I am different—because I'm a Christian?

If you are modeling Jesus Christ at your school, then you could answer these questions in the affirmative. Your school is an important training ground for living the extreme life of a Christian. You must decide who you are living to please. Is it your friends, or your friend Jesus?

And here's another thought before we move on: If you are having a hard time living for Christ at school, then you will have a hard time living for Christ in the world. *How you model Christlikeness at school today is more than likely how you will model Christ in the future when you are an adult.*

Live for Christ today,
and you will live for Christ tomorrow.

Turning Your Life into an Extreme Adventure

Recently I had lunch with one of my buddies from high school. We hadn't seen each other in a l-o-n-g time, so we had a lot of catching up to do. We asked each other about our classmates and where they are today. It was very sad to hear that most of our guy friends had not thought much about going somewhere that counts. They had not focused their efforts along the way on the extreme adventure ahead. And, as a result, they were never prepared for any journey.

I don't want that for you, my friend! I don't want people in the years to come to be sitting around talking about you and all the adventures you could have had...but didn't because you weren't prepared.

Don't get me wrong—I realize that formal education isn't everything, and that some people can survive without the training they receive at school...but not many. And I also want to say again that your relationship with Jesus Christ is the most important part of your development. If you do nothing else but grow in your knowledge and faith in Jesus and "grow in favor with God," then you are one of the best of students.

But let me quickly add that it's helpful for you to get the training that will help you to grow "in favor with man." This will make you a complete man—a man who is ready for the rough seas, the high wind, and the pitching decks of life. This will make you a man who can take it to the extreme—a man after God's own heart!

Tough Decisions for Today

Look at your life this past week. How many hours do you think you spent in these three areas:

> hours just playing around (with computer games, watching TV, etc.)

> hours with friends

> hours on homework

What do your answers reveal about your priorities? Are there any changes that need to be made?

Are there any other Christians at your school? What would it take for you to get together with several of them for accountability and to pray for one another so that your witness would be noticeable and bold?

The Cutting Edge

Present yourself to God as one…
who correctly handles the word of truth.

—2 TIMOTHY 2:15

What do these proverbs teach you about the importance of wisdom and knowledge, and what do they teach you about how they are gained?

Proverbs 2:6

Proverbs 4:5

Proverbs 4:7

Proverbs 9:10

List three things you can do to grow in wisdom and knowledge.

9

Making the Right Choices About Friends

A friend loves at all times,
and a brother is born for a time of adversity.

—PROVERBS 17:17

As I sit here writing this chapter, I can see Mount Rainier off in the distance. Even though we live almost 50 miles away from this landmark peak in the state of Washington, and even though it's August, the snow-capped crown of this 12,000-foot extinct volcano is still enormously impressive. Because Mount Rainier is so accessible, climbers routinely travel from all over the world to hike it.

But unfortunately, just as routinely, there are radio and TV reports of deaths, injuries, falls, or stranded climbers. In most cases there is a happy ending. That's usually because there was an experienced climber, a buddy, along to help when his fellow climber got into trouble. The fact that the injured climber was saved was, in part, due to having chosen a skilled climbing companion.

"So what does mountain climbing have to do with developing the right friendships?" you might ask. Well, just as it is critical to have an experienced climber with you as you scale the slopes of a mountain, it's critical to have the right friends as you scale the slopes of life. You might not think there is even a remote similarity between Mount Rainier and your life, but hopefully before we are through with this chapter, you will change your mind.

Being a Friend

You may be one of those guys who have never met a stranger. You can talk to others and make friends easily. But most men are not that fortunate. For them—and maybe for you—it's not easy to find a good friend. Whether you have many friends or few, however, I'm sure you'll agree that friendship is a two-way street. It's been said, "If you want a good friend, be a good friend." So for us, we need to begin by talking about what makes us a good friend.

In the Bible, God gives us guidelines on how to be a good friend. As you read through these biblical nuggets of wisdom, decide in your mind and heart what kind of friend you must be. Also pick out what a friend—a *real* friend—does and does not do.

Whoever would foster love, covers over an offense,
but whoever repeats the matter separates close friends
(Proverbs 17:9).

A friend loves at all times,
and a brother is born for a time of adversity
(Proverbs 17:17).

One who has unreliable friends soon comes to ruin,
but there is a friend who sticks closer than a brother
(Proverbs 18:24).

Wounds from a friend can be trusted,
but an enemy multiplies kisses (Proverbs 27:6).

Do not forsake your friend (Proverbs 27:10).

As iron sharpens iron,
so one person sharpens another (Proverbs 27:17).

Yes, But How?

How do you find friends and friendships that last? As we said earlier, developing the right friendships starts with you—*you* need to be the right kind of friend! So, here are some key guidelines on becoming a "super friend." If you practice these suggestions, you will find people wanting to be your friend.

1. *Be growing spiritually*—As you looked over the characteristics of a good friend in the verses above, you probably realized that you need help—God's help! How can you find the right kind of godly friends? First, desire to be godly yourself. (Sound familiar? That's what we covered in the first section of this book.) If you desire to grow spiritually and know God more intimately, you will look for friends who also share a love for God.

This is the kind of mutual friendship that was shared between Jonathan, the son of a king, and David, the future king (1 Samuel 18–20). Be sure to read about their friendship in more detail later. For now, though, here's a great description of their friendship:

Jonathan saw that David viewed life from the same divine perspective.... And when he saw this, his soul

reflexively clung to David's. Here was a man whose
heart beat with his! [9]

That's the way it is with real friendships. No, you won't
always agree on every issue. But you will share a mutual view on
what the Bible says about those issues. The author I just quoted
summed it up this way:

> You assent to the same authority.
> You know the same God.
> You are going in the same way.
> You long for the same things.
> You dream mutual dreams. [10]

Do you want godly friends? Then, as I said, be growing spiritually. Also use the five characteristics above as a checklist as you
go about the process of choosing friends. Then you will find what
you are looking for.

2. *Be yourself*—Don't try to be someone you're not. And
don't try and imitate the personalities and actions of the "pop-
ular" kids at school, especially if they don't jive with what you
are reading in your Bible.

Here's something else to think about. How do you end up
acting when you are pretending to be someone else? It's rather
artificial, right? You are uncomfortable with those you are trying
to be like, and you make others feel the same way. The harder you
try, the more artificial you become, and the more people you drive
away. So be genuine. Being comfortable with who you are helps
others to feel comfortable when they're around you. Just be yourself, and God will bring like-minded people to be your friends.

That's what happened with David. He had just defeated the greatest enemy of his nation, and he was brought before King Saul. Jonathan, Saul's son, had been there and witnessed David's courage. And being a man of courage himself (1 Samuel 14:1-13), Jonathan admired and wanted to be a friend to David (1 Samuel 18:1).

Keep this in mind: If you honor God with your life, others who are committed to godly principles will seek you out.

3. *Be loyal*—Loyalty is a must if you are to be a good friend. I'm sure a "fair-weather" friend has hurt you at one time or another. You know how that feels, so don't turn around and be disloyal to someone else. As you look at the friendship between Jonathan and David, you see this kind of mutual loyalty. Jonathan stood up to his father, King Saul, in defense of his friend David. And David kept his promise to Jonathan to look after his family in the future when he became king (1 Samuel 20:14-17).

How loyal are you to your friends? Are you "a friend who sticks closer than a brother" (Proverbs 18:24)? In addition to sticking up for your friends, do you keep secrets? Or do you gossip and listen to gossip about a friend?

4. *Be understanding*—You must understand that your friend's life doesn't revolve around you. That doesn't make him any less of a true friend. That just means that there are times when a friend spends time with others, like his family or church group or even other friends, like the people on a sports team or those involved in a mutual activity. Because you understand, you can support your friends and their other commitments and responsibilities. You can encourage them in their relationships and responsibilities.

You can pray for your friends and even volunteer to help out whenever you can.

5. *Be honest*—One of the benefits of a true friendship is honesty. The Bible puts it this way—"Wounds from a friend can be trusted....and the pleasantness of a friend springs from their heartfelt advice" (Proverbs 27:6,9). You and a true friend should be committed to pulling each other up toward God's goals and standards for young men who desire to honor God. You need to be a trusted friend that tells it like it is.

And don't get upset when your friend takes on this same role to help you grow in an area where you need help. Honesty works both ways, you know!

6. *Be careful with the opposite sex*—I've wanted to get to this subject since we started this chapter, but first it was extremely important for us to lay a foundation for friendships in general—biblical friendships, right friendships, godly friendships. With this foundation in place, we're now ready for just a few thoughts (we'll devote more time to this topic in the next chapter). Every principle we have covered so far can apply to friendships with girls. You need to be friendly to everyone, but also be cautious when it comes to girls. The three things you will really need to watch out for in your conduct and speech with the opposite sex are...

> being too friendly,
> being too physical, and
> being alone together.

We'll talk more about this most important subject soon.

7. *Be an encourager*—Anyone can tell your friends ten things that are wrong with them or with their actions. But an encourager

tells people what is right about them. Let's go back a minute to the friendship between David and Jonathan. Their relationship was based on their mutual love for God. So how did they encourage each other? The Bible says that when it was evident David was targeted for murder (by Jonathan's father, King Saul), "Jonathan went to David…and helped him find strength in God" (1 Samuel 23:16).

The best way to encourage your friends is to help them find strength in the Lord, through the Scriptures and through praying together. But you can also give compliments. And be sure you are specific with your praise. Praise your friends for something special you appreciate about them, something you see in their conduct or admire in their character.

As an encourager, you want to strengthen and further your friends' relationships with God. As they grow spiritually, you will be challenged to grow as well. It's Proverbs 27:17 in action: "As iron sharpens iron, so one person sharpens another." That's what encouragement is all about—challenging each other to grow. And you benefit when your friends grow. Why? Because your friends are your future. You become what your close friends are!

8. *Be involved*—You and I have to make willful decisions about keeping and growing friendships. It takes time, care, and effort to make sure our good friendships are sustained and kept growing. You can't neglect a friendship and expect it to be alive and healthy. No, you must work at being a good friend—a phone call, an email, an invitation to go with you and your family to a ball game.

The apostle Paul told his friends in Philippi, "I have you in my heart" (Philippians 1:7). Do you have your friends in your heart? Are you involved in their lives?

9. *Be a pray-er*—One of the greatest blessings you offer to your friends is the gift of prayer. Everyone struggles with trials every day. Your friends face issues that they may never share with you. You'll never know all the battles that are being fought in your friend's life and home. So you pray.

And what do you pray? Pray for their spiritual growth, their relationships, their schoolwork, and their involvement at church and other activities. Apart from parents or a youth worker, you might be the only one praying for your friend!

So be faithful, be frequent, and be fervent in your prayers. You never know when you just might be the true friend whose faithful prayers helped your friend resist temptation, make a right decision, endure something difficult, or even excel in greatness.

Turning Your Life into an Extreme Adventure

Do you remember how we began this chapter? We talked about choosing a partner or a team for a mountain-climbing adventure. A wise mountain climber will pick companions who are as good as or better than he is. And you know why, don't you? That way, if he gets into trouble, he has someone who can help save him.

It's the same way with friendships. You should desire and seek out friends who are going in your same direction spiritually—friends who will either "pull you along" in your goal of Christ-likeness, or "pull you up" to even higher levels of Christianity. And where do you find this type of friend? You usually find them at church or in other Christian groups or functions.

Fellow believers will be there when you need spiritual help or encouragement. They will be a great resource for accountability to God's standards. Your friendships with other solid Christian guys will mirror the one enjoyed by Jonathan and David. In short, your best friends should be strong, like-minded Christians who help you to think your best thoughts, do your best deeds, and be your best self.

So as you go about the business of finding and developing friendships, make sure *you* are developing the qualities you are looking for in a friend. Set the highest standards for yourself, and don't settle for less than God's highest standards in anyone you would label a "best friend."

Never forget that you and other young men are climbing an extremely difficult mountain. Sure, it's an extreme adventure, but it's also extremely demanding. Your friends will come to places where, as a climber, they could stumble and fall into a deep crack or crevice. Be the best friend a fellow climber could choose. Be someone he can trust. And make sure you, too, choose your climbing friends with great care. You never know what might happen during the climb toward the goal, toward godliness, toward the top. You will want others beside you who are strong enough to help keep you from falling.

Tough Decisions for Today

Review the list of the nine guidelines for being a good friend. Which areas are you especially strong in as a friend, and what makes you say so?

Review the list again. Did you discover an area (or two) where you need improvement? What is it, and what do you plan to do about it?

Are you convinced yet about the importance of picking your friends wisely? Why or why not?

The Cutting Edge

Present yourself to God as one…
who correctly handles the word of truth.

—2 TIMOTHY 2:15

Read about Jonathan and David in 1 Samuel 14:6-14.
Describe the kind of warrior Jonathan was.

Read 1 Samuel 17:32-37 and 48-51. Describe the kind
of courage David possessed.

Now read 1 Samuel 18:1-4; 19:1-6; and 20:1-42.
How did the friendship between Jonathan and David
develop, and what was it based on?

What lessons in friendship can you learn from David
and Jonathan?

10

Fighting the Battle Against Temptation

Put on the full armor of God,
so that you can take your stand.

—EPHESIANS 6:11

War is hell!"

That's what I often heard from my dad, who lived by this slogan as a soldier and fought in Germany during World War II. But a generation later, as I sat in a classroom at Fort Bragg, North Carolina, I was hearing it again…and beginning to feel the full force of the words, "War is hell!"

How did I come to be sitting in a military briefing room at Fort Bragg? My Army Reserve unit was called up for active duty during the Bosnian crisis in the 1990s. We were on our way to Germany to take over the duties of a regular Army hospital unit that had been deployed to the battlefront in Bosnia.

So there I sat, receiving a combat briefing. I was listening to instructors lecture on land mines, snipers, mortar attacks, chemical warfare, and other extreme threats. It was clear that the Army wanted our group to be prepared for any and every kind of danger we might face in battle.

Life Is a Battle

Living the Christian life is a battle, too! (And if you don't think so, then you just might not be living the Christian life very successfully!) As we've already noted, Jesus Himself told us, "In this world you will have trouble" (John 16:33). That trouble for us men comes in a variety of packages. And, like my Army instructors, God wants us to prepare for the inevitable battle... which takes us back to chapters 1–5 of this book. As you might remember, these first five chapters covered the importance of properly preparing yourself to handle the priorities in your life. One of those priorities is being ready to face and defend yourself against the temptations the enemy will throw at you.

God's Take on Temptation

Most of us don't need to make a list of the temptations we struggle with every day, do we? Hopefully, your list is a short one. But as you mature and are exposed to more of the world and its sinful allurements, your list of temptations will probably expand greatly.

In the Bible, God gives us His take on what we can look forward to as we do battle with temptation and sin. Galatians 5:19 starts us off by informing us that "the acts of the sinful nature are obvious"—and then the list reads:

> ...sexual immorality, impurity, lustful pleasures, idolatry, sorcery, hostility, quarreling, jealousy, outbursts of anger, selfish ambition, dissension, division, envy, drunkenness, wild parties, and other sins (Galatians 5:19-21).[11]

Pretty awful, isn't it? So how in the world can a young man after God's own heart get a handle on these temptations and fight the battle against them? The fact that you are concerned at all is the first step in fighting the battle. The second step is realizing that you have choices to make.

Two Men, Two Choices, Two Paths

There are myriads of thoughts penned on the importance of choices. Have you heard this one?

> Little choices determine habit;
> habit carves and molds character
> which makes the big decisions.

Or how about this one?

> Choice, not chance,
> determines human destiny.

To see these truths lived out, meet two men…who made two choices…that led to two paths and two destinies.

Man #1 was Cain—the firstborn son of Adam and Eve. Cain and his brother, Abel, brought gifts to God, and they received two different responses from God. Abel and his gift were pleasing to God, but Cain and his gift were not (Genesis 4:1-8).

What happened when God judged against Cain's gift? Cain had two choices for his response—he could either come before God and humbly ask forgiveness for himself and the nature of his gift, or he could become angry with God because of the rejection.

Unfortunately, Cain chose the less noble response. He became angry with God. God then warned Cain about his wrong attitude and its potential consequences by saying, "Sin is crouching at your door; it desires to have you, but you must master it" (verse 7).

Two men, two choices, two paths. What wrong choice did Man #1 make? Cain chose to allow sin to master him and failed the test for handling temptation God's way. His jealousy toward his brother Abel and God's acceptance of Abel's gift caused him to sink deeper into sin and ultimately to murder his brother. In the end, Cain's inability to handle temptation disqualified him from God's blessing and from any influence for good with his life. His choice led him down a path of destruction.

Man #2 was Jesus—who lived thousands of years after the days of Cain and Abel. This man, too, faced temptation. After 40 days of fasting, He was in a physically weakened state and was tempted by Satan in three different areas of life. With all three temptations, Jesus fought back, quoting the Word of God (Luke 4:1-12). Jesus chose to withstand the temptations. He passed the tests perfectly and walked the path of influence. By choosing the path that led to the cross, He impacted the entire world. His path led to your salvation and mine. The tale of these two men looks like this:

Two Men:	Cain	Jesus
Two Choices:	gave in to sin	withstood temptation
Two Paths:	murdered his brother	saved many
Two Results:	self-destructed	influenced many

Your Choice, Your Path

The choices of these two men give you and me some very sobering lessons on the importance of dealing with temptation and sin. (Did you notice that I put temptation before sin? Temptation is not sin. Cain was tempted—sin was "crouching at the door." He *could* have chosen to resist the temptation and therefore not to sin, but he didn't. Jesus was tempted, but *did* resist the many temptations.)

The pressing question is, How about you? How are you dealing with your thoughts, and your temptations? Where are your choices leading you? What direction are you headed? I'm sure you can identify with me—and all other men—in these struggles. And I'm sure you, like me, are not always pleased with the way you handle (or fail to handle!) temptation.

Take heart, my fellow struggler. God has provided a way for us to stand up under the struggle of temptation and choose to move down the path of victory. The Bible says, "No temptation has overtaken you except what is common to mankind. And God is faithful; he will not let you be tempted beyond what you can bear. But when you are tempted, he will also provide a way out so that you can endure it" (1 Corinthians 10:13).

God's Provision for Your Temptations

The fact of temptation is real—very real! And the good news is that God has made provision for your temptations.

First, God has provided a new law—A law is a fixed way in which things work. For instance, the law of gravity says that anything heavier than air will fall toward the earth. That means if you jump off a ten-story building, you will fall to your death. But what if there is a law that counters the law of gravity, such as the law of aerodynamics? This law allows a 747 jumbo jet, filled with hundreds of people and weighing many tons, to fly.

In the same way, when you and I come to Christ, God counters the law of sin and death—a law that gives us no choice but to die separated from Him for eternity. But when we come to a saving knowledge of Jesus Christ, we come under the influence of a new law—the law of the Spirit of life in Christ (Romans 8:2). This new law sets us free from the bondage of sin. We now have the power of a new law to choose to resist temptation.

Second, God has provided a guide—A guide is someone or something that leads you through unfamiliar territory and keeps you from getting lost. Jesus promised He would give believers a "guide" to live in them and always be with them. That guide is the Holy Spirit, who lives in all believers and guides them into all truth (John 16:13). When you and I came to Christ, this promise of Jesus became true for us. As a result you now have your own guide—the Holy Spirit—who leads you throughout all of life and through all of the situations you will ever face.

Third, God has provided a guidebook—God has also given you your very own personal guidebook, the Bible. Everything you need to know about life and godly living is presented to you in God's Word (2 Peter 1:3). This guidebook gives you the answers to deal with every temptation you will ever face!

Fourth, God has provided guides—God has provided other believers to help you overcome the temptations of this world. That's why it is so important to be involved in a local church and youth group. There you can find others who can hold you account-able and guide you with wise counsel. I am personally thankful to God for the many men who have served as faithful, caring mentors to me. These "soldiers of the cross" were committed to watching over my spiritual growth on the battlefield of life.

Now, you may be saying, "But Jim, you don't know my situation. You don't know the pressures I'm under—pressures at school, pressures at home, and pressures from my peers. I *can't* help but succumb to temptation. No matter how hard I try, I *can't* seem to overcome these particular sins!"

Well, you're right. I don't know what specific issues you are struggling with. But I do know that you are not alone. Temptation is universal. The Bible says it is "*common* to mankind" (1 Corinthians 10:13). That means I can say that you and I and all men struggle with the same temptations and sins. That's the bad news.

But the good news is that God has provided a way out, an escape and victory with these four resources—

> a new law—life in Christ,
> > a guide—the Holy Spirit,
> > > a guidebook—the Bible, and
> > > > guides—wise counselors.

You have the ability to withstand the temptations that confront you in your daily living. Statements of *I can't* no longer apply to you. Now, in Jesus Christ, it's *I can!* Paul tells us to "be strong in the Lord and in his mighty power" (Ephesians 6:10).

So the next time you are faced with an opportunity to sin (like in the next millisecond!), remember, "I can do all this through him who gives me strength" (Philippians 4:13). God has given you the *I can* to deal with that temptation. But you must supply the *I will*. It's your choice. Your path and your character are at stake! No choice is a small choice. And no choice is a meaningless choice.

Yes, But How?

Is there a way out? As we have just seen, there is! God has provided resources to assist you in dealing with temptation and sin. But He is asking you to do your part. He is asking you to "be strong in the Lord and in his mighty power. Put on the full armor of God, so that you can take your stand against the devil's schemes" (Ephesians 6:10-11). So as you do your part, here are some practical choices you can make to fight the battle of temptation.

- *Pursue godliness*—This is what God is talking about when He says to "put on the full armor of God." God's armor will protect you in the battle when you pursue a life of godliness. "Pursue righteousness, faith, love and peace" (2 Timothy 2:22). How do you put on God's armor? By reading your Bible, praying, worshiping with God's people, and being accountable to your youth leaders and strong Christian friends. These are God's resources for the battle, for war!

- *Avoid places where you might be tempted*—Stay away from TV programs, movies, or music that go against God's standards or fan your sexual emotions. Stay away from magazine racks with sensual covers on display. Stay away from those who talk or brag about sin. Stay away from being *alone* with someone of the opposite sex. Paul's advice to his young disciple is very appropriate for you and me, too: "Flee the evil desires of youth" (2 Timothy 2:22).

- *Avoid people who might tempt you*—In the last chapter we discussed choosing the right kind of best friends—those who will pull you up or along. But I didn't mention that there is a third kind of "friend." This kind of friend is one you need to avoid like the plague! You must avoid having the kind of friend who "pulls you down." Be careful of buddies from the past and friends in the present who have a lower standard than you want for your life.

The Christian life is hard enough to live without this type of person in your life. So do yourself a favor and drop these kinds of friends, especially if you aren't strong enough to resist their low standards. God said it best... and to the point: "Do not be misled: Bad company corrupts good character" (1 Corinthians 15:33).

- *Avoid allowing your eyes to roam*—Most of the temptations that you encounter come to you through your eyes and are sexual—billboards, magazines, movies, TV, and what you see at the swimming pool or on the beach—or anywhere on a hot summer day! Jesus taught that you can actually commit sexual sin in your heart by just looking at a girl or woman with lustful thoughts (Matthew 5:28). So determine to do what Job did! He actually "made a covenant with [his] eyes not to look lustfully at a young woman" (Job 31:1).

- *Pursue a godly approach to dating*—I told you we would eventually get back to the subject of girls, didn't I? Well, dating is certainly a hot topic in Christian circles—do you or don't you date? Should you or shouldn't you date? If yes, at what age? And do you call it dating or courting? And if you do go on a date, do you go as a couple or in a group? The discussion could go on and on...and it probably will!

So let's start by asking your parents what they think you should do. Then, let's ask your youth leaders about dating. What do they say? And now, let me give you my "two cents" of advice to add to your decision-making process. Why not set a high standard? Why not...

—*Choose* not to date all the way through high school. I have made my own observations as well as asked a variety of people (teachers, youth pastors, parents, counselors) about this vital subject. And all agree that few, if any, couples who date in high school actually end up marrying each other. So what's the point of dating? You've probably already noticed that most of your temptations as a young man are (and will continue to be) sexual temptations. And dating without a godly purpose has no point. All it does is take you on an emotional roller coaster ride that can end up getting you into sexual trouble.

—*Choose* instead to focus on group activities, preferably church activities. Use this time to observe how godly young ladies act. What is their focus? Where is their heart? (Remember, just like you are trying to choose godly guy friends, it's vital to choose godly girls for your friends.)

—*Choose* to involve your parents. Ask your parents what qualities you should look for in the girl that you would eventually "date" or "court" for the purpose of marriage.

—*Choose* to remain morally and sexually pure, no matter what! You must make this commitment now, before you begin dating. And you must make it again and again before each date you go on (whenever you finally decide to start the dating process). Remember, this is a spiritual choice. Are you going to follow the path of the world, or Jesus?

Turning Your Life into an Extreme Adventure

My dear younger brother, let's agree to fight the battle against temptation, especially sexual temptation, with our eyes wide open! You are sitting in the briefing room and this is the lecture on war—the war against temptation and sin. These are the cold hard facts: Temptation is ongoing. As long as you are alive and breathing, you will be dealing with every temptation that the enemy and the world can throw at you. The battle will rage in every area of your life for as long as you live.

The question is, Will you allow God to fight your battle for you through the resources He has given you? Or will you try to go it alone? If you try to go it alone, you will fail. I repeat, *you will fail!* So choose to look to God for help. You have His Word. You have His Spirit. You have the weapon of prayer. You have wise counselors and people who care about you. Through God and His arsenal of resources, the victory is yours.

Thanks be to God!
He gives us the victory
through our Lord Jesus Christ.

—1 Corinthians 15:57

Tough Decisions for Today

Just for today, monitor your thoughts and conversations. Try to pinpoint any changes that need to be made. What verses in this chapter were the most helpful to you?

Are there any areas of your life where you are failing to resist temptation? Ask God for forgiveness, and then choose to invite Him to go to battle with you in this area. Is there a more mature man who can hold you accountable? What steps can you take to ask him for help?

The Cutting Edge

Present yourself to God as one…
who correctly handles the word of truth.

—2 TIMOTHY 2:15

Using your Bible, look at the following scriptures. Write what each one teaches about your physical purity and why it is important to God…and to you (hint: some have multiple answers).

1 Corinthians 6:19—

1 Corinthians 6:20; 1 Peter 1:19—

1 Thessalonians 4:3-5—

If your purity is this important to God, what are you going to do about protecting it?

11

Reaching Out to Others

Always be prepared to give an answer
to everyone who asks you
to give the reason for the hope that you have.

—1 Peter 3:15

As a Christian do you ever feel like you are outnumbered? That you are surrounded by giants? That you are small and insignificant? That you have very little, if any, Christian support at your school because your teachers and fellow students have different and opposing beliefs? That you are outmanned and the battle seems impossible to win?

Well, if you have ever had any thoughts like these, you are not alone. Ten other "special ops" warriors had similar concerns more than 3,000 years ago. You can read about their self-doubt in Numbers chapter 13, but for now, let me give you the short version.

The "Grasshopper Complex"

God had brought His people out of Egypt with signs, wonders, and miracles—the ten plagues, the parting of the Red Sea, and the provision of food and water in the desert. The people of Israel had witnessed the great power of God. And now they were ready to go into the Promised Land. But as one last final preparation, Moses sent his 12 best men—the best of the best—to spy out the land. "Operation Promised Land" took 40 days. And at the end of that time, the men returned to give their reports.

Ten of these mighty men reported that the land was a beautiful place, filled with lots of good things…but there was just one problem: The land was also filled with giants who lived in walled cities! The people were so b-i-g that the spies felt like grasshoppers compared to them. The ten warriors concluded that it would be a terrible mistake to try and conquer the land. The giants were just too big and too strong!

Now, didn't I tell you that you are not alone in your feelings about the overwhelming odds you face at your school and in your neighborhood? These ten men were, as I said, the best of the best…and they too were fearful with what was out there.

But is that the end of the story? No! Remember, I said Moses sent out *12* men. Let's see what the other two men, Joshua and Caleb, had to say when they reported in:

> If the LORD is pleased with us, he will lead us into that land, a land flowing with milk and honey, and will give it to us. Only do not rebel against the LORD. And do not be afraid of the people of the land, because we will devour them. Their protection is gone, but the LORD is with us. Do not be afraid of them (Numbers 14:8-10).

"Do not be afraid of them" was the cry of Joshua and Caleb! Why? Because, as they stated, "The LORD is with us." They stood up under the pressures from both their own people and from the giants in the land.

God is asking you and me to be a witness for Him in our world. Let's not view our world as impossible to conquer. Let's not develop a "grasshopper complex." Let's instead stand tall with these two brave men, Joshua and Caleb, and let God fight our battles and win our victories.

Yes, But How? (Developing a Battle Plan)

Guys often tell me they don't know how to share their faith, or they don't think they know enough Bible or theology to be able to tell someone else about their faith in Christ. For these reasons, they shy away from the many opportunities that come up for reaching out to others with the good news of Jesus Christ. Do you feel this way, too? You are not alone.

It's true that skills and knowledge are important and that you should learn more of God's truth and be equipped to share your Christian faith. But it's not necessary for you to be a theologian before you can share about the most significant aspect of your life with those who are willing and eager to listen.

Sharing Your Testimony
The Example

I don't know how long you've been a believer in Christ, but you've probably heard your pastor or youth leaders talk about "sharing your testimony." Basically, your testimony is your story of how you became a Christian. To show you just how simple it is to share your testimony, I want to point you to the story about the demon-possessed man in Mark 5:1-20.

The short version of the story is that a man was tormented by a whole host of demons. Jesus, in His mercy for this poor man, cast the demons out of him and sent them into a herd of pigs, which then ran down a hill into a lake and drowned.

You can imagine how thrilled this tortured man was to be free of the demons. So he immediately asked Jesus if he could follow Him. You might think Jesus would say, "Sure, come follow Me and learn some theology. Sit at My feet and let Me tutor you for a few years until you are ready to share your testimony with others."

No, Jesus simply told the man to "go home to your own people and tell them how much the Lord has done for you, and how he has had mercy on you" (Mark 5:19). Basically, Jesus told the man to go home and share his testimony! You see, even as a new believer, this man already had all he needed to testify of his experience with Jesus.

And what happened? What were the results of this man's obedience to Jesus? The Bible tells us "the man went away and began to tell in the Decapolis [his home region] how much Jesus had done for him. And all the people were amazed" (verse 20).

The Results

What was the impact of this man's changed life? I believe we see it later on in Mark 7:31–8:9. Here we read that Jesus was moving through a Gentile region outside of Israel. Jesus had not been in this area before, nor was He well known there. But amazingly, when Jesus arrived at this remote place, He was met by a crowd of about 4,000 men (not to mention many women and children) ready and waiting to hear His message!

Where did these people come from? I personally believe the man in Mark 5 had done exactly what Jesus told him to do. I believe he had obediently told people how much Jesus had done for him. I believe he had simply shared his testimony, and those people showed up in a faraway place to see Jesus and to hear His message for themselves.

The Specifics

My young friend, your personal testimony of Jesus' work in your life is the greatest and most powerful tool you have for reaching others for God. Why? It's about *your* experience with Jesus Christ! It's personal. So no one can argue against it. And you can never say the wrong thing. Also, the fact that it happened to you makes it more meaningful to the people who hear you describe it.

Your personal testimony can be broken down into three parts:

Part one—*What my life was like before I met Jesus Christ*

Part two—*How I met Jesus Christ*

Part three—*What my life has been like since meeting Jesus Christ*

Now, take a moment to think back over your past. What are the circumstances that led up to your acceptance of Christ as Lord and Savior? What changes or differences have you—and hopefully others—seen in your life since you became a Christian? Using this three-part breakdown for your personal testimony, try to briefly note what happened to you. (To help you out here, I've included a worksheet or outline for you at the end of this chapter.)

Once you've written your notes, you are ready to carry out the apostle Peter's exhortation in 1 Peter 3:15: "Always be prepared to give an answer to everyone who asks you to give the reason for the hope that you have." So send up a prayer of thanks to God for your relationship with Him through His Son. And ask Him to give you an opportunity to share the reason for your hope—*your personal testimony*—with someone this week.

Building Bridges

I once heard the story about a high-level official in a foreign government who enrolled his non-Christian son in a Christian college in America. There was a great excitement among the students about who might have the opportunity to share the gospel with this young man and possibly see him come to Christ. Would it be the senior class president? The star athlete? The campus chaplain?

Well, the foreign student did come to Christ. But everyone was surprised about who God used as His messenger. It was Tom, just an average guy. You would never pick Tom out of a crowd as someone with unusual skills or witnessing abilities. Later, when someone asked him what happened, he said, "I simply built a bridge between my heart and his, and then Jesus walked across it."

Developing friendships. Building bridges. Hey, *this* is what it means to develop a heart for reaching others! You and I don't need to be pastors...or Bible experts...in order to witness. No, but we do need to earn the right to be heard by those around us...like Tom did.

What are some ways that you can build bridges that will help carry the message of Jesus Christ from your heart to the hearts of others? Here are some suggestions to get you started or help you to continue building bridges. (We could even call this Bridge Building 101!)

Live your Christian witness—As you consistently try to live your life for Jesus Christ, your schoolmates and neighbors will see Him at work in you through...

- your positive attitude

- your commitment to purity
- your speech
- your work habits
- your church involvement
- your friendliness

Ask God to give you the strength to "walk the walk" so that you can "talk the talk."

Pray for unbelievers—Salvation is *God's* job; witnessing is *our* job. And so is prayer. You and I are to build bridges…and at the same time, we are to pray for God to walk across those bridges into the hearts and lives of others. So:

1. Pray for specific individuals…your family members at home, your relatives, your schoolmates, and your friends.
2. Pray for "open doors"…to share your testimony just like Paul did (Colossians 4:3).
3. Pray for wisdom…about what you communicate (Colossians 4:5-6).
4. Pray for God to overrule…your fears and give you great boldness (Ephesians 6:19).
5. Pray faithfully…for others to know Christ.

As you look over this "prayer" list again, think about George Mueller. He lived more than 100 years ago in England and ran an orphanage for hundreds of children. Mr. Mueller began to pray for the salvation of five personal friends. After five years, one of those friends came to Christ. After ten years, two more became saved. For 25 years he continued praying for the other two, and then the fourth one became a Christian. Until his death, he did not cease to ask God to save the fifth man. A few months after George Mueller died, Friend #5 was saved!

The moral of this story? Never give up on others! Never stop praying for their salvation.

Pay attention to the interests and hobbies of others—One of the best ways to build bridges is to learn about the interests of those you are making friends with. Are you prepared to take up a new hobby in order to build a bridge to someone? To try a new activity? (Tennis, anyone?)

Relate the Bible to current issues—There's never been a better time to discuss the questions others have about the future... and the present! Just pick up any newspaper. Listen to any news program. Every day there are issues facing us that cry out for an explanation...and God has it! Look for opportunities to relate what the Bible has to say about current events in the world. Speak up and show others the Bible's relevance to the latest national or world crisis.

Show genuine interest in others—Human nature is pretty much marked by selfishness. Don't you agree? People care much more about themselves than they do about anyone else. So show some genuine interest in others. Remember names. Pay attention to favorite sports teams and heroes, the concerns and interests of your unbelieving friends. Go out of your way to show them that you care. Then others will begin to see you as a friend...and see Christianity as something desirable.

Meet non-Christians in the middle—What do I mean by "in the middle"? You will meet very few unbelievers at your church or Christian youth group. Sure, you might meet visitors who wander in off the street or who are brought to church by a friend or neighbor. But for the most part, the unbelievers are *out there*—in your neighborhood…at school…at the baseball field or skateboard park. So meet them in the middle. Meet them wherever the two of you are involved.

Invite unbelievers to participate in your hobbies and interests—In addition to taking an interest in the hobbies of unbelievers, you can also invite them to join you. Do you play ball? Then invite someone to join you and your friends for a friendly game of "tag football" on the vacant lot near your house or on your lawn. Or maybe you play chess…or water ski? As other guys observe your life "up close and personal" on the field of competition or enjoying a hobby, they will see more of who you are not only as a person, but also as a Christian.

Giving an Answer for Your Hope

Not long after I began teaching at Talbot Seminary in Southern California, I was asked by my department head to attend a seminar on student life in Chicago. As I listened to one of the "learned" speakers who had a theological degree from a famous university, it wasn't long before I realized this man didn't have a clue about what it meant to have a personal relationship with Jesus Christ.

So, during one of the lunch breaks, I sat with this "Doctor" and started a conversation about salvation, and the gospel message, and the fact that those who don't become Christians are condemned to an eternity without God. I'll never forget this religious professor's response....

"Well, what about the heathen in Africa?"

His question brings up one of the most common fears most people have about sharing their faith. They worry, "What if someone asks me a question that I can't answer?"

Well, the chances of that happening aren't too great, for there are only about seven basic questions that non-Christians generally ask as they grapple with the truth of the gospel. And would you believe it—this well-educated man asked the Number One question on the list!

A question for you—Are you like most guys, afraid of the questions that might come your way after you've built the bridges and after you've developed the friendships? Well, cheer up. Questions are a good thing. Hopefully there *will* be questions! You should welcome them. Questions are a good sign that the person might want to hear more, and that God might be working in his heart!

Witnessing for Christ is not a one-way street. And reaching out is not a monologue, but a dialogue. Evangelism is listening to other people. It's understanding their fears and questions. And it's seeking to give biblical answers.

What we as Christians need to do is have enough compassion to find out the questions our peers have and then go to the Bible for answers. As I mentioned a moment ago, there are only about seven basic questions (or objections) that unbelievers have and ask about. I've listed them here. And after each objection, I've provided the most basic scriptures that will help you with the answers. My prayer is that you have developed the kinds of friendships with others that will make them feel comfortable asking you one—or even all—of these questions.

Seven Basic Objections to the Gospel

1. What about the heathen who have never heard the gospel?
   (Answer: Psalm 19:1; Romans 1:18-20)

2. Is Christ the only way to God?
   (Answer: John 14:6)

3. Why do the innocent suffer?
   (Answer: Romans 5:12)

4. How can miracles be possible?
   (Answer: John 1:1,14; 3:2)

5. Isn't the Bible full of errors?
   (Answer: 2 Timothy 3:16; Hebrews 1:1-2; 2 Peter 1:20-21)

6. Isn't the Christian experience merely psychological?
   (Answer: Acts 9—the conversion of Paul; Romans 5:8-10)

7. Won't a good moral life get me to heaven?
   (Answer: Galatians 2:16; Titus 3:5; James 2:10)[12]

Turning Your Life into an Extreme Adventure

Earlier, we talked about making friendships with the kinds of Christians who will help pull you along and pull you up. So you might be wondering why we're now talking about building bridges and reaching out to unbelievers. When we speak of evangelism and reaching out, we are not talking about "evan-gelistic dating" with an unbeliever or "infiltrating" a group of unbelievers and becoming so much like them that you lose your distinctiveness as a Christian. We're talking about the kind of friends you develop in the classroom, in the gym, as a member of a sports team or musical group. You and your non-Christian friends will have interests and physical goals in common, but obviously you won't share the same spiritual goals.

But wouldn't you like them to know the same joys you know as a Christian? That's why you must take on the task of building bridges and making friendships with unbelievers—so you will have an opportunity to "give an answer to everyone who asks you to give the reason for the hope that you have" (1 Peter 3:15). The challenge is great. The adventure is extreme. But the rewards are eternal for those who come to Christ through your witness—both verbal and nonverbal. Show people that you really care. Turn your fears and concerns over to the Lord. "Do not be afraid of the people of the land….the Lord is with [you]" (Numbers 14:9).

Tough Decisions for Today

Fill out this worksheet or outline for developing your personal testimony. Keep each part to about three or four sentences.

Part One—*What my life was like before I met Jesus Christ*

Think back over your life. What were some of the circumstances that led up to your acceptance of Christ as Lord and Savior?

Part Two—*How I met Jesus Christ*

Describe the people who were faithful to be available at the time of your spiritual birth. What happened?

Part Three—*What my life has been like since meeting Jesus Christ*

What changes or differences have you—and hopefully others—seen in your life since you became a Christian?

The Cutting Edge

Present yourself to God as one…
who correctly handles the word of truth.

—2 TIMOTHY 2:15

Ask God…

—to give you an opportunity to share the reason for your hope—*your personal testimony*—with someone this week.

—to encourage you to "go home to your family and tell them how much the Lord has done for you" (Mark 5:19). Share with those closest to you—family, friends, and neighbors—what Jesus has done for you.

Part Three

Going for
the Gold

12

Pressing for the Prize

Straining toward what is ahead,
I press on toward the goal to win the prize
for which God has called me heavenward
in Christ Jesus.

—Philippians 3:13-14

Remember my trip to Australia that I mentioned earlier? I called it a challenging trip—an extreme adventure. Well, I've been on other crazy ventures as well, and on one of them, when the dust finally settled afterward, I had traveled through seven countries in 17 days!

The day-by-day log of the trip went something like this: Sightseeing on a double-decker bus in London. Straddling a camel at the base of the pyramids in Egypt. Floating in the mineral-laden waters of the Dead Sea in Israel. Walking "the street called Straight" in Damascus, Syria. Climbing the ancient stairs of the Coliseum in Rome. Riding a donkey between sheer red-rock walls in a narrow crevice leading to the deserted city of Petra in Jordan.

And on the final night of that adventure, before heading for home, I was in Athens, Greece, witnessing an impressive light show while hearing about the glories of ancient Greece. The announcer's voice boomed out to the thousands of onlookers the history of how the Greeks had started the Olympic games more than 2,000 years ago. He dramatically described how the modern-day Olympics we now enjoy every four years are just an extension of those ancient events.

Paying the Price

Well, several years have passed since that memorable evening in Athens. So vivid was it that I experience many of the sights and sounds of Greece all over again when I watch the Olympics on TV! Even if you don't like sports, you can't help but be drawn into this greatest of all sporting events in the world.

And, as you watch the games, the commentators give out a lot of information about the different participants. They talk about how hard these Olympians work and the price they pay to prepare to even qualify for their sport, let alone participate in the Olympics.

Many of today's competitors practice 12 to 16 hours a day, six days a week—for years!—to run a ten-second race, to swim a lightning-speed lap, to perform a triple-with-a-twist gymnastics move, to contort over the pole-vault bar, to guide a horse to jump a man-high brick wall. These people are fiercely dedicated in their desire to compete—and win! Therefore, they pay the price.

I have to tell you, as I listen to the commentary and watch the breathtaking, strenuous competition that takes place during the Olympics, I can't help but wonder about my own commitment to run the race I'm in—the Christian race. To swim in the pool I'm in—the world. To press for the prize I'm to seek—"the prize for which God has called me heavenward in Christ Jesus" (Philippians 3:14). To give my utmost—for His highest. To "go for the gold"—for eternity! Do I have an Olympian's mentality? Am I motivated and driven to complete some task, or to train or prepare for some event or assignment or ministry? Do I have the will, the desire, to pay the price and press onward for the prize and hopefully win?

What about you? How's your commitment to "go for the gold"? Oh, not for Olympic gold, but for the gold of another kind—the gold of being the best you can be? The gold that has you doing your best at every event, activity, work chore, homework assignment, whatever—all to please your Lord?

That's what we want to talk about in this chapter—what it's going to take for you to be a man after God's own heart, to be God's man today...which will give you great momentum for being God's man tomorrow. Look over these principles that others have followed in their quest for God's gold, and let them help you, too.

Principle #1: Be Diligent

The apostle Paul was an amazing guy. He truly modeled this principle of diligence. Even with his all-out life of ministry, he still had time to train many young men. One of those men was Timothy. We first meet Timothy in Acts 16:1. He's a young man just entering the ministry. Then some 15 years later, we again meet up with Timothy, who by this time is the pastor of the church in Ephesus.

When Paul wrote to Timothy about his pastoral duties, he said, "Do your best to present yourself to God as one approved, a workman who does not need to be ashamed" (2 Timothy 2:15). In other words, Timothy was to make every effort—to give his all—to do his best. Why? So he wouldn't have any cause to be ashamed...not before his mentor, Paul, but before God, the Person Timothy was really serving. Timothy was told to be diligent at what he was called to do—to preach and teach—so as not to shame the Lord.

Friend, God is asking you and me to develop this same heart of diligence and to be the best at whatever we do, too.

Principle #2: Do Your Best

Over the years I've traveled to India 15 times for ministry. India is a fascinating and unique country with a great mass of people who need Jesus Christ. Because of my deep interest in India, my eye was drawn to this story that speaks of doing your best at whatever God calls you to do.

> A missionary from India told about an army officer who stopped to have his shoes shined by a poor Indian boy on the street. The lad launched into his task with such enthusiasm and vigor that the man was utterly amazed. Instead of an ordinary, slipshod performance with an all-too-eagerly outstretched hand for a tip, the boy worked diligently until the leather sparkled with a brilliant luster.
>
> The officer asked, "Why are you taking so much time to polish my boots?"
>
> "Well, sir," was the reply, "last week Jesus came into my heart and now I belong to Him. Since then, every time I shine someone's shoes, I keep thinking they're His, so I do the very best I can. I want Him to be pleased!"

This young man demonstrated a desire to do his best. Is the same true of you? Are you willing to go so far as to shine shoes to the glory of God...or take out the trash or clean up your room and please the One who died in your place? Because of what Christ has done for you and me, how can we do less than give Him our best?

- We give God glory *when* we do our best.

- We represent the Lord Jesus, *therefore* we do our best.

- We serve the Lord and not men, *so* we do our best.

- We provide a living model of our risen Savior *while* we do our best.

- We fulfill God's purpose *as* we do our best.

Principle #3: Be a Servant

For eight years I worked as a pharmaceutical salesman. During that time, I participated in a management training program at the company's corporate headquarters. In those meetings, we aspiring managers were put into specific sales situations and then asked to solve the problems. You can probably imagine the scene as each of us attempted to demonstrate to the bosses that we were superior management material!

While this training was hard work, it was needed. Everyone needs to learn to work with others to solve problems. And everyone needs to learn to assume leadership roles and be accountable when things go wrong. And those of us who are Christians should go a step further: We should not only seek to excel at all that we do and at all times, but we should also seek to be a servant as well. That may seem contradictory, but it can be done! As Christians, we are to approach *everything* we do in life as a servant, whether at home with parents, at school with friends and teachers today, or tomorrow as you get further training in school or enter the work world. And Jesus will give us the guidance we need in this matter of servanthood.

Looking to Jesus' example—The Lord Jesus Himself modeled the kind of servant you and I—and every man after God's own heart—ought to be. A week or so before His death, two of Jesus' disciples, James and John, asked for the best positions in the kingdom. Hear Jesus' reply:

> You know that the rulers of the Gentiles lord it over them, and their high officials exercise authority over them. Not so with you. Instead, whoever wants to become great among you must be your servant, and whoever wants to be first must be your slave—just as the Son of Man did not come to be served, but to serve, and to give his life as a ransom for many (Matthew 20:25-28).

Do you want to be great—in a good sense, that is? True excellence is not determined by being Number One, by being at the top. Jesus was the greatest leader of all time…and yet He was a servant to all.

Following Jesus' example—How? By being a servant to the people around you. After all, serving others is one of the marks of a godly man. To become a servant…

- live with a servant's attitude, which means that you…

- live to promote others,

- live to praise others,

- live to encourage others,

- live to ask, not tell, and

- live to give, not take.

Friend, you have a choice about your attitude.

—You can live with an attitude of *taking from* others whatever is needed for your own well-being. This attitude perceives other people—your parents, your teachers, your friends—as existing to serve you. Or...

—You can have the attitude that says, "What can I *put into* this relationship?" This better attitude—the attitude of a servant—seeks to promote others, to make their lives better. Contributing positively to the lives of others is the role of a servant.

Principle #4: Be a Learner

Remember the epitaph on the scientist's tombstone in chapter 1? "He Died *Learning*." Well, friend, that should be our motto as well. You and I should die learning. Unfortunately, many young men have this backwards. Their motto is, "I would rather die than learn!" They dislike school of any kind and can't wait for graduation so they can get on with "real life." Or they exert only the minimum effort necessary to get by. And sadly, tomorrow they will wake up and have very limited career options because they're not continuing to learn.

Now, I want to be quick to say that I know many a guy who has made it to the top levels of his profession or trade with a minimum of formal education. But if you look closely at these men, you'll find that each one has continued his education—maybe not in a formal way, but informally. In other words, they have continued to learn, and that's the reason for their great progress.

That's what I mean by being a learner. Learning isn't limited to schools and textbooks. No, learning has to do with ongoing development. I see learning this way:

- Learning is a state of mind, an attitude.

- Learning is progressive—it builds upon itself.

- Learning is not dependent on your IQ.

- Learning does not distinguish between nationalities.

- Learning does not require a formal classroom education.

- Learning does not always offer a degree.

- Learning does not require a degree.

- Learning is commanded in the Bible (2 Peter 3:18).

- Learning is a way of life for a man after God's own heart.

Here are a few simple suggestions for continuing to learn for a lifetime:

Learn to read—Most men read very little...or not at all. In fact, surveys show that only about five percent of all Christian books are bought by men. Brother, if this is true, we are heading in the wrong direction when it comes to reading! Reading is the window to all learning. Reading exposes you to the entire globe and to the knowledge and experiences of others. Therefore, reading should become a passion for us!

When the godly men at my church started helping me in my desire to become a man after God's own heart, I noticed they were always reading. Desiring to grow and wanting to follow in their footsteps, I asked for suggestions on what I should read. And you can do the same, too. Ask your youth leaders at church for a book list so you can begin your own journey in learning.

And don't forget—the first book you want to read is the Bible. Read it a little at a time from cover to cover, over and over, for the rest of your life. (For help on this, you'll want to see the reading schedule in the back of this book.)

Learn to ask questions—Everyone has something to teach you. So approach every person as your teacher. They are an expert on *something*. Find out what that something is, and then learn it from them. Make an effort to ask the questions that will expand your understanding of their knowledge.

Learn from the experiences of others—It's been said that the person who depends upon his own experiences has very little material to work with. So, again, ask questions and seek to learn from the experiences of anyone who is willing to teach you. And, although you can't pose questions of the great people of the past, you *can* read their biographies. You can learn from their successes, and you can learn to avoid their mistakes.

And, I repeat, don't forget your Bible. The Bible is the best of all books for learning from the experiences of others. Just think how much we've already learned from the successes…and mistakes…of David! The Bible should be your primary textbook for life and for learning.

I pray you will never stop learning! And to ensure that you learn, you should do it every day. So, each day, ask yourself…

- "What new thing can I learn *today?*"

- "Who can I learn from *today?*"

- "How can I be stretched in some aspect of my life *today?*"

Turning Your Life into an Extreme Adventure

Are you grasping the importance of these years of your life right now? The habits and disciplines you acquire today and during the next few years will lay the foundation for the rest of your life. How can you turn your life into an extreme adventure? You can choose today—and every day—to make an effort to begin the adventure, to get onto the fast track, and to press for the prize...or you can choose to waste these critical years.

Today Matters is the title of a best-selling book. And I hope you believe it! To me, the truth of this title means:

- Today's good decisions will give you greater opportunities tomorrow.

- Today's good habits will give you greater discipline tomorrow.

- Today's good attitudes will give you a greater desire for winning the prize tomorrow.

Obviously, there's more—much more!—that could be said about pressing for the prize as you strive to be a man after God's own heart. But for now, I'll leave you with the words on the next page about becoming "a winner."

A Winner

- A Winner respects those who are superior to him and tries to learn something from them; a Loser resents those who are superior and rationalizes their achievements.

- A Winner explains; a Loser explains away.

- A Winner says, "Let's find a way"; a Loser says, "There is no way."

- A Winner goes through a problem; a Loser tries to go around it.

- A Winner says, "There should be a better way to do it"; a Loser says, "That's the way it's always been done here."

- A Winner shows he's sorry by making up for it; a Loser says, "I'm sorry," but does the same thing next time.

- A Winner knows what to fight for and what to compromise on; a Loser compromises on what he shouldn't, and fights for what isn't worth fighting about.

- A Winner works harder than a loser, and has more time; a Loser is always "too busy" to do what is necessary.

- A Winner is not afraid of losing; a Loser is secretly afraid of winning.

- A Winner makes commitments; a Loser makes promises.[13]

Tough Decisions for Today

Read again the story of the boy who shined shoes. What can you do today to exhibit a higher level of diligence?

List your acts of service during the past 24 hours. What do they reveal about your attitude as a servant? What can you do today to exhibit a higher level of service?

The Cutting Edge

Present yourself to God as one…
who correctly handles the word of truth.

—2 TIMOTHY 2:15

Read Genesis 39:1-6. Describe Joseph's situation and how Potiphar rewarded Joseph's diligence, excellence, and service.

Read Genesis 39:20-23. Describe Joseph's new situation and how the warden rewarded his diligence, excellence, and service.

What verses show you the connection between God's blessing and Joseph's diligence?

13

Integrity Makes a Difference

Samuel said to them,
"The LORD is witness against you,
and also his anointed is witness this day,
that you have not found anything in my hand."

—1 SAMUEL 12:5

In 1517, a 34-year-old German priest named Martin Luther became outraged that people were being taught that freedom from God's punishment of sin could be purchased with money. These "indulgences" were outlined in an edict from Pope Leo X. In response, Luther wrote 95 statements, in which he criticized the Pope, explaining that the sale of these "get-out-of-hell-free passes" were biblically incorrect. He addressed other problems as well, and nailed these statements to the door of Castle Church at Wittenberg.

On April 18, 1521, Martin Luther, knowing full well the serious nature of his summons, appeared as ordered before The Diet of Worms, a general assembly of the Catholic Church in the town of Worms in Germany. He was presented with copies of his writings laid out on a table. Then he was asked if the books were his, and whether or not he stood by their contents. Luther confirmed he was their author. Then he requested time to think about the answer to the second question. He prayed, consulted friends, and gave this response the next day:

> Unless I am convinced by the testimony of the Scriptures or by clear reason (for I do not trust either in the pope or in councils alone, since it is well known that they have often erred and contradicted themselves), I am bound by the Scriptures I have quoted and my conscience is captive to the Word of God. I cannot and will not recant anything, since it is neither safe nor right to go against conscience. May God help me. Amen.

Martin Luther is also quoted as saying: "Here I stand. I can do no other." But regardless of the full extent of his statement, the effects of the now-famous Ninety-Five Theses were huge. Luther's integrity—his willingness to stand true to his beliefs—was the spark that ignited the great Protestant Reformation.

Integrity: Don't Leave Home Without It!

What's the one thing you like and value most about your close friends? Sure, you like the way they make you laugh, or the way they "have your back" when things get sticky. But if you stopped and gave this some hard thought, you would probably say, "It's trust." The best kind of friend is someone you can trust. When he says he will do something, then you can count on him to come through. There's a name for that quality—it's called *integrity*.

We all admire and respect people who act with integrity. Like Martin Luther, they aren't afraid to stand for the truth or to do what is right. And in the same way you appreciate integrity in others, you should cultivate it in your own life. Integrity is something you want to be known for both at home with your family and when you leave your house.

Because integrity is such an essential trait for a young man after God's own heart to possess, let's define what it is, and how we can develop it.

The Meaning of Integrity

Integrity, when applied to...

1. a ship's hull, describes what makes a ship seaworthy.

2. an airplane's wings, describes what will ensure an airplane's ability to stay in the air even in the most severe weather.

3. a chemical compound, describes the exactness of the formulating process.

So, whether it's a boat, or an airplane, or a chemical compound, integrity insures that the object or substance can be trusted to fulfill its intended purpose.

Integrity, when applied to a person, means...

1. being truthful, trustworthy, having conviction,

2. being steadfast, adhering to a strict moral or ethical code, and

3. being unimpaired in a direction or focus.

Integrity should be what you want for yourself now, and what you are willing to strive to keep for the rest of your life. Integrity can be summed up simply as doing the right thing for the right reason even when no one is watching.

This is why integrity is admired in people, especially a leader. People want to follow someone into battle or into a business venture or into the future whom they can trust to do right by them. They are willing to trust a person of integrity with their life, with their financial future. Why? Because they can be assured that such a person will keep his promises and follow through on his commitments to them.

You might not see yourself as a leader right now, but having or developing a life of integrity will set you apart from others, and as a result, you will have opportunities to lead people naturally by example.

The Nature of Integrity

How are you when it comes to science? I personally have always been drawn to science and took lots of science classes in high school and college. One of the principles of science is that every substance acts in a certain way. This is called its "nature." Integrity too has a way or manner of conducting itself—its nature.

Integrity enforces moral convictions. Integrity gives resolve to a person's actions. It is unmoved by any immorality surrounding it. A person who displays integrity will choose…

1. honesty over deceit,

2. fairness over injustice, and

3. a willingness to abide by rules and regulations even when those rules are disregarded by others.

Integrity protects itself. Integrity knows that its standards have been hard-fought—and won. It also knows that with only one mistake or indiscretion, a person's trustworthiness can be forfeited. Therefore, it establishes a hedge of accountability for its protection.

You might not think so, but you have areas of weakness. Even if you can't think of the one or two areas where your Christian armor is a little thin, just ask the devil. He would be glad to explore those areas with you! Or you can take a shortcut and ask your parents. They would be glad to help point out areas of your life that could be improved upon.

When you are willing to admit you are not perfect, you will purposefully surround yourself with opportunities for accountability that help you to protect your integrity. You will make sure there are safeguards in your life that prevent against character failure and keep your integrity intact.

How can you make yourself accountable?

- Accountability comes first from the ultimate source of accountability, God's Word. If you are faithful to read and study the Bible, God the Holy Spirit will expose areas of your life that are in need of change. God reveals "them to us through His Spirit. For the Spirit searches all things, yes, the deep things of God" (1 Corinthians 2:10 NKJV).

- Accountability also comes while you are living at home. You should thank God that He has given you parents, who will help establish boundaries for you. You must also listen with a grateful heart when the youth leaders at your church let you know when you are veering off course. "As iron sharpens iron, so one person sharpens another" (Proverbs 27:17).

- Accountability comes with a teachable spirit. Many young men ignore the cautions and concerns of those in authority. "Instruct the wise and they will be wiser still; teach the righteous and they will add to their learning" (Proverbs 9:9).

Integrity creates a value system. What do I mean by "value system"? This is a set of beliefs that you adopt as your standard to guide your behavior as you live your life. The world has become one big "gray area," which means there are few or no rules, standards, or values—everything has become relative. In other words, people just do whatever they think is okay. Many young people—and old ones too—take comfort in what is called "situational ethics." The situation determines their ethic, or their response. Actions and conduct are often based on the present climate of your surroundings. But that's not how integrity works. Rather than ask, "Is my behavior acceptable to my surroundings?" integrity asks, "Is my behavior consistent with my set of Bible-based values that are fixed and unmoved and will never change?"

Christian integrity is based on the clear-cut value system presented in the Bible. Things are either right or wrong, good or bad, black or white.

You, as God's young man, must live in a world that rejects the Bible's value system. But that shouldn't keep you from living out God's standards of holiness and truth. You cannot impose your beliefs on the people around you, but you can impress others by staying faithful to a value system that has God and His Word at its core.

Integrity makes the harder choices. Integrity requires having the courage to choose the higher moral ground. Integrity understands the consequences of wrong decisions, and therefore agonizes to make the right choices. Compromise, on the other hand, is easy. It takes little or no thought to conform to a low standard. Any weak or unprincipled person can take the easy way out.

God's man, however, adopts a noble code of ethics. For you, as a Christian, that code is the Bible. Even though people may resist your code, they will admire you for your focus and your tenacity in upholding your standard.

Integrity draws people to a higher standard. Integrity is a garment that can be worn by anyone. You might be thinking, *Who will ever notice if I do what's right, no matter what the cost? What difference will it make if I have integrity? I'm just a young guy!* Because integrity is such a rare quality, believe me, people of all ages will notice.

In spite all the complaining you hear from your friends about the rules in their homes and at school, people function better when they are part of something that is anchored in established rules. Your integrity reminds your friends of these rules. Your integrity, by its very nature, will pull others toward a higher standard. Your actions will promote a higher level of behavior. By showing integrity, you can model and direct people to a better way of living.

Men in the Bible Who Modeled Integrity

Now let's see how integrity shows itself in the lives of three great men of the Bible—Samuel and Daniel from the Old Testament, and the apostle Paul from the New Testament.

Samuel—This priest was one of the Bible's greatest models for integrity. From his earliest years he devoted himself to serving God's people. It wasn't easy. After all, he did grow up in the temple and witnessed the corrupt conduct of the two sons of Eli, the head priest. These sons were immoral. They did not respect God or the people's sacrifices. The bottom line: The sons of Eli had no integrity, and Samuel was exposed to that.

Yet in spite of these two negative examples, Samuel became a man with integrity, a man after God's own heart. As the end of his exemplary life drew near, he stood before the people one last time and reminded them of his behavior. Hear what marked him with integrity:

> I have been your leader from my youth until this day. Here I stand. Testify against me in the presence of the LORD and his anointed. Whose ox have I taken? Whose donkey have I taken? Whom have I cheated? Whom have I oppressed? From whose hand have I accepted a bribe to make me shut my eyes? If I have done any of these things, I will make it right (1 Samuel 12:2-3).

In the very next verse, the people affirmed Samuel's integrity and conduct: "You have not cheated or oppressed us...You have not taken anything from anyone's hand" (verse 4). Then they added God Himself to their list of witnesses: "He is witness" (verse 5).

Samuel's integrity was based on his desire to honor God and serve His people. His honesty and personal goodness permeated every area of his life. His integrity determined how he handled his possessions, how he dealt with the people, and how he treated the weak and needy.

Samuel's example calls you to hold to this same standard of integrity. Whatever your age, and whatever direction you set for your future, let your desire for personal integrity shine forth in what you do each and every day. When you commit yourself to living with integrity, you will be a man others will gladly follow!

Daniel—This prophet is a super example of integrity. Success has its rewards, but also its dangers. Because Daniel was so good at what he did (a positive!), other leaders were envious of his achievements (a definite negative!). The Bible assesses his abilities in this way:

> Now Daniel so distinguished himself among the administrators and the satraps by his exceptional qualities that the king planned to set him over the whole kingdom (Daniel 6:3).

What was the response of his fellow-administrators?

> At this, the administrators and the satraps tried to find grounds for charges against Daniel in his conduct of government affairs (verse 4).

What skeletons did they find in Daniel's closet? Because Daniel was a politician, his enemies thought they would have no trouble coming up with some type of wrongdoing in his personal or professional life. They thought Daniel was as corrupt as they were. But, much to their alarm, "they were unable to do so. They could find no corruption in him, because he was trustworthy" (verse 4).

What did Daniel's enemies finally do? They said, "We will never find any basis for charges against this man Daniel unless it has something to do with the law of his God" (verse 5).

Daniel's character was made clearly evident when these jealous men examined his life. Integrity will stand up under the scrutiny of those who bring a charge against it.

The apostle Paul—Here is another true servant of God. On his way back to Jerusalem at the end of his third missionary journey, Paul stopped at a seaport called Miletus. There he asked the leadership from the church that he had planted at Ephesus to join him for a brief visit. First Paul gave them encouragement (see Acts 20:13-32). Then he reminded them of his conduct during the three years he was with them, saying,

> I have not coveted anyone's silver or gold or clothing. You yourselves know that these hands of mine have supplied my own needs and the needs of my companions. In everything I did, I showed you that by this kind of hard work we must help the weak, remembering the words the Lord Jesus himself said: "It is more blessed to give than to receive" (Acts 20:33-35).

Paul led by example. He didn't use other people to satisfy his own personal needs. Instead he worked to care for himself and the others on his team.

Turning Your Life into an Extreme Adventure

Looking at these three great examples of integrity, you can't help but see that integrity is a heart issue. And that's the secret of integrity—it's an inside job! Integrity is a matter of the heart: "A good man brings good things out of the good stored up in his heart" (Luke 6:45). There is no such thing as having "some integrity." Either you have integrity...or you don't. Either you are a man of integrity...or not.

How can you make sure that integrity is alive and well in your heart today and therefore your life? How can you ensure that integrity will continue on into adulthood? Here are some steps you can take to strengthen your heart's resolve as you build and polish your integrity.

Step 1: Realize the value of integrity. Integrity defines who you are as a person. It also refines you and guides your actions. It puts a wall of protection around you and keeps you walking down the correct path—God's path. A wise man highly values his integrity.

> The end is never as satisfying as the journey.
> To have achieved everything but to have done so without
> integrity is to have achieved nothing.[14]

Step 2: Choose and use the truths of Scripture as your standard of integrity. Stand with Martin Luther in his resolve: "I am bound by the Scriptures...My conscience is captive to the Word of God. I cannot and will not recant anything, since it is neither safe nor right to go against conscience."

Step 3: Examine your heart. Go to God daily with a desire to have the searchlight of His Spirit examine you. Don't trust your own heart when it comes to self-examination. Only God can give a correct reading of the condition of your heart. "The heart is deceitful above all things and beyond cure. Who can understand it?" (Jeremiah 17:9). Therefore cry out to God, "Test me, LORD, and try me, examine my heart and my mind" (Psalm 26:2).

Step 4: Evaluate your decisions. Cautiously and prayerfully appraise your every decision, however large or small. Take time to carefully look at your choices. Then, based on the truths of Scripture, decide what you must change in your behavior to align your life more closely to God's standards. Weigh each decision: Does this choice affirm my integrity? If not, obviously it's out! Let David's resolve be yours: "May the words of my mouth and the meditation of my heart be pleasing in Your sight, LORD, my Rock and my Redeemer" (Psalm 19:14).

As a young man after God's own heart, integrity should be at the very core of your being. Open your heart to God and let Him shape you with His Word. Then allow the Holy Spirit to guide and guard your every thought and decision.

The strength of your character depends on the strength of your integrity. Someone may take your life, but they can never take your integrity. Only you can relinquish your integrity. So stand guard over your integrity at all costs! Live your life so you can pray, "Vindicate me, LORD, for I have led a blameless life. I have trusted in the LORD and have not faltered" (Psalm 26:1).

A person is not given integrity.
It results from the relentless pursuit
of honesty at all times.[15]

God's Purpose in You

*When David had served God's purpose
in his own generation, he fell asleep.*

—Acts 13:36

What's that guard doing standing at attention out there in the middle of the palace lawn?" This was the question a lady in our tour group asked the guide. The lady immediately followed with a second question: "What's his purpose?"

These two questions were on everyone else's minds too. But with the exception of the lady, everyone was too shy or hesitant to ask. Nobody wanted to ask what might be perceived as a dumb question.

Of course there was a perfectly good reason for that guard standing out there on the grounds of that Old English castle. No one just stands guard without a purpose, right?

As in most castle tours, there are always stories about how certain traditions got started. Well, the story behind this lone guard was interesting. It was said that many years ago, a queen was having a lawn party and reception. As the guests starting arriving, the queen was inspecting the palace lawn and to her horror, she spotted a single large weed standing in the middle of her beautifully manicured lawn. Thinking quickly, she motioned for one of the palace guards to come and stand on the weed throughout the reception. Unfortunately, no one told the captain of the guard the reason for the queen's request, and over the years, guards continued to stand at attention on that exact spot. The weed is long gone, but to this day there stands a guard at full attention—but for no real purpose.

David, a Man with a Purpose

Acts 13:36 brings us full circle in the life of David. Do you remember how our study began with God's epitaph that David was a man after His own heart (verse 22)? David started out with very few of the qualifications that are typically expected of a king—he was still a young teenager caring for the family sheep when he was anointed to rule over Israel. But David had a heart for God, and that was what God wanted most. As 1 Samuel 16:7 says, "The LORD does not look at the things people look at. People look at the outward appearance, but the LORD looks at the heart."

As we have often noted in this book, David experienced lapses in his walk with God. But unlike the ruler before him, King Saul, there always came a point in time when David turned back to God with great remorse and sorrow. This attitude of repentance was what made David useful to God. This sterling quality is what made David a man after God's own heart—a man who, according to Acts 13:36, "served God's purpose in his own generation."

Following David's Footsteps

I'm so thankful that you have stayed with me all through this book. I am praying that you have come to understand that in everything, God looks at the heart. Your relationship with God has to do with your heart and your heart's desires. Like David, you probably have lapses. We all do! But you also have a choice. You can choose to please yourself and ignore God. Or you can please God and obey Him.

Do you desire to obey God? All through this book you have been challenged to develop a heart for God and the things of God. Whose example will you follow? Don't follow after Saul's example! Instead, follow in David's footsteps. Give God your whole heart and obey Him. Then you, like David, will be a man God can—and will—use.

Pursuing God's Purpose

I admitted early on that I was somewhat puzzled about God's epitaph for David because of David's serious lapses. But God had a life purpose for David. David willingly, though falteringly at times, followed God's purpose for his life. His heart for God allowed him to be used mightily by the Lord in his own generation. He was used of God in spite of his shortcomings.

And guess what, my young friend: God has a life purpose for you too! What an incredible opportunity you have available to you. You, like David, have a purpose. Will you live out your own purpose, or God's? Wouldn't you want it to be said of you that you are serving the purpose of God? My guess is that you desire this as much as I do. What man of God wouldn't want to fulfill God's grand purpose for his life?

Well, you can make God's purpose for you a reality. How? Simply by living out God's priorities. You can't do anything about the past. But starting today, you can personally and positively affect this generation—your generation. And this will happen naturally as you live out God's priorities for your life.

Where Do You Go From Here?

In the personal letter at the beginning of this book, I stated that my goal is to simply and clearly lay out some of God's priorities for you. These priorities come from the Bible, and as such are trustworthy pursuits. They have inspired countless young men to do whatever was required of them as God's men whether they were still in school or starting out in a new job or serving in the military at sea, in the air, or on land. And now I'm trusting that you too desire to make these priorities your own.

But it's not enough to just live out the principles and priorities in this book before your own generation, even though doing that will have a great impact. Why should it stop there? Why not extend your impact by influencing the *next* generation of younger men—maybe even your own boys, if you have children someday? Wouldn't that be special? Are you interested? If so, you must take the next step—share with others what you have learned and what you will continue to learn in the weeks, months, and years ahead.

The information and experiences you gain are valuable for living your life right now. But what if all your learning and experiences were to be passed on? Think of the additional people who could benefit!

There is a term for this process of passing on information and experiences—it's called *mentoring*. In the Christian community, we call this *discipleship*. This is one of the important lessons I have learned since I first wrote this book nearly 10 years ago: You and I must pass on to others the things we are learning!

The Concept of Mentoring

In a mentoring relationship, a person with more knowledge or experience helps to guide someone with less knowledge and experience. This involves more than just offering sporadic help. It means developing an ongoing relationship that includes regular dialogue, instruction, and challenges.

The word *mentor* has an interesting history. It seems that in the eighth century BC, the poet Homer wrote in his major Greek work, *The Odyssey*, about a man named Mentor. Mentor was a friend of the warrior Odysseus. When Odysseus went off to fight in the Trojan War, Mentor was left in charge of Odysseus's household. Mentor was also charged with teaching, tutoring, and protecting Telemachus, Odysseus's son. Mentor was faithful to "mentor" Telemachus until his father returned many years later.

In our Christian churches today, the idea of mentoring fits perfectly with this biblical concept of discipleship as illustrated by Mentor. Anyone who is an experienced advisor, supporter, teacher, coach, or tutor takes on the title of discipler. This is how the apostle Paul described that process:

> The things you have heard me say in the presence of many witnesses entrust to reliable people who will also be qualified to teach others (2 Timothy 2:2).

Paul, a Master of Discipleship

Eight hundred years after Homer and *The Odyssey*, but before the idea of mentoring became a fashionable concept in our modern society, the apostle Paul, like Mentor, was a discipler of men. But unlike Mentor, who trained only one young boy, Paul was an advisor and trainer of many. He took what he knew of God's Word and God's will and passed it on to others.

Here's an exciting thought: Anytime you read one of Paul's 13 epistles, you are being discipled by this amazing man! And as you read, you can't help but notice some of the people Paul affected with his life, his knowledge, and his experiences. As we look at two of Paul's disciples, be thinking of who you could be influencing by simply sharing what you are learning.

Timothy—We have spoken often about Timothy in past chapters, which further validates the effectiveness of discipleship. Timothy is probably the most well-known of Paul's pupils. Paul met young Timothy on his first missionary journey and may have even led him to faith in Christ. He called Timothy "my true son in the faith" (1 Timothy 1:2). Paul worked with Timothy for 15 years, and we can see the effect Paul's mentoring had on Timothy's life. Timothy had matured to the point that he became the pastor of the flagship church in the whole region of Asia Minor at Ephesus.

Titus—Here's another man Paul poured his life into. Titus, like Timothy, was given more and more responsibility as he matured in the faith. Titus was the one commissioned by Paul to go to the island of Crete to choose and train up leaders for the churches. (See the book of Titus.)

Passing On the Baton

I started running while in high school, and I have continued to jog for years. I wasn't one of the faster runners on my school team, but I had endurance, so I ran the distance races. Most events in track and field are individual competitions, and I ran all of my races as a sole competitor against runners from other schools. This meant I alone was responsible for my performance.

On occasion, however, I would run as part of a relay team consisting of four runners who must pass a baton from one person to the next. In these medley events, I was no longer a sole competitor. Instead, I was part of a team. I had to run my part of the race well, and then carefully hand the baton to the next runner.

As I see it, mentoring or discipleship is like a relay race. You run your leg of the race as well as you can. You do the best you can with your knowledge and experiences. And then you carefully pass the baton of information and experiences on to the next person.

You may be asking, "How can I be qualified to pass on anything? I'm just a teen guy!" Well, for one thing, if you have read to this point in this book, you can meet with one of your buddies and go through this book together. Then you can find another guy and go through the same process again. As time passes, hopefully this won't be the only book you will read with regard to your spiritual growth. Any good book that will help you grow as a Christian is a book you can study together with other guys. The idea is to pass on what you are learning to others.

Turning Your Life into an Extreme Adventure

Is Paul's focus on pouring his life into others giving you any ideas about the effect you can have on others even as a young man? Are you beginning to understand the impact of passing on the baton by mentoring or discipling other guys at your church or school?

Purpose, prepare, and plan to pass on the priorities we have discussed, the priorities that relate to your relationship with God, your parents, the people in your church, and even those who are not Christians. This focus will serve as a great beginning toward fulfilling God's purpose for your life. I challenge you as I challenge myself: Seek God's help in carrying out His purpose by reading your Bible, finding someone to disciple you, and then passing on what you are learning. Make God's desire your desire—live out His priorities.

And what's more, your striving toward fulfilling God's purpose will have a ripple effect on others for generations to come as you are faithful to pass on to others what God is teaching you. You will etch your commitment to living a life after God's own heart on others, and this living epitaph will be true of your life:

_____ (your name)
is a man after God's own heart
who is living out the purpose of God.

Extreme Spiritual Workout Schedule:

A One-Year Daily Bible Reading Plan

January

Genesis

❏	1	1–3
❏	2	4–7
❏	3	8–11
❏	4	12–15
❏	5	16–18
❏	6	19–22
❏	7	23–27
❏	8	28–30
❏	9	31–34
❏	10	35–38
❏	11	39–41
❏	12	42–44
❏	13	45–47
❏	14	48–50

Exodus

❏	15	1–4
❏	16	5–7
❏	17	8–11
❏	18	12–14
❏	19	15–18
❏	20	19–21
❏	21	22–24
❏	22	25–28
❏	23	29–31

❏	24	32–34
❏	25	35–37
❏	26	38–40

Leviticus

❏	27	1–3
❏	28	4–6
❏	29	7–9
❏	30	10–13
❏	31	14–16

February

❏	1	17–20
❏	2	21–23
❏	3	24–27

Numbers

❏	4	1–2
❏	5	3–4
❏	6	5–6
❏	7	7–8
❏	8	9–10
❏	9	11–13
❏	10	14–15
❏	11	16–17
❏	12	18–19
❏	13	20–21
❏	14	22–23
❏	15	24–26
❏	16	27–29
❏	17	30–32
❏	18	33–36

Deuteronomy

❏	19	1–2
❏	20	3–4
❏	21	5–7
❏	22	8–10
❏	23	11–13
❏	24	14–16
❏	25	17–20

❏	26	21–23
❏	27	24–26
❏	28	27–28

March

❏	1	29–30
❏	2	31–32
❏	3	33–34

Joshua

❏	4	1–4
❏	5	5–7
❏	6	8–10
❏	7	11–14
❏	8	15–17
❏	9	18–21
❏	10	22–24

Judges

❏	11	1–3
❏	12	4–6
❏	13	7–9
❏	14	10–12
❏	15	13–15
❏	16	16–18
❏	17	19–21

Ruth

❏	18	1–4

1 Samuel

❏	19	1–3
❏	20	4–6
❏	21	7–9
❏	22	10–12
❏	23	13–14
❏	24	15–16
❏	25	17–18
❏	26	19–20
❏	27	21–23
❏	28	24–26

❑	29	27–29
❑	30	30–31

2 Samuel

❑	31	1–3

April

❑	1	4–6
❑	2	7–10
❑	3	11–13
❑	4	14–15
❑	5	16–17
❑	6	18–20
❑	7	21–22
❑	8	23–24

1 Kings

❑	9	1–2
❑	10	3–5
❑	11	6–7
❑	12	8–9
❑	13	10–12
❑	14	13–15
❑	15	16–18
❑	16	19–20
❑	17	21–22

2 Kings

❑	18	1–3
❑	19	4–6
❑	20	7–8
❑	21	9–11
❑	22	12–14
❑	23	15–17
❑	24	18–19
❑	25	20–22
❑	26	23–25

1 Chronicles

❑	27	1–2
❑	28	3–5

❑	29	6–7
❑	30	8–10

May

❑	1	11–13
❑	2	14–16
❑	3	17–19
❑	4	20–22
❑	5	23–25
❑	6	26–27
❑	7	28–29

2 Chronicles

❑	8	1–4
❑	9	5–7
❑	10	8–10
❑	11	11–14
❑	12	15–18
❑	13	19–21
❑	14	22–25
❑	15	26–28
❑	16	29–31
❑	17	32–33
❑	18	34–36

Ezra

❑	19	1–4
❑	20	5–7
❑	21	8–10

Nehemiah

❑	22	1–3
❑	23	4–7
❑	24	8–10
❑	25	11–13

Esther

❑	26	1–3
❑	27	4–7
❑	28	8–10

Job

- [ ] 29   1–4
- [ ] 30   5–8
- [ ] 31   9–12

June

- [ ] 1   13–16
- [ ] 2   17–20
- [ ] 3   21–24
- [ ] 4   25–30
- [ ] 5   31–34
- [ ] 6   35–38
- [ ] 7   39–42

Psalms

- [ ] 8   1–8
- [ ] 9   9–17
- [ ] 10   18–21
- [ ] 11   22–28
- [ ] 12   29–34
- [ ] 13   35–39
- [ ] 14   40–44
- [ ] 15   45–50
- [ ] 16   51–56
- [ ] 17   57–63
- [ ] 18   64–69
- [ ] 19   70–74
- [ ] 20   75–78
- [ ] 21   79–85
- [ ] 22   86–90
- [ ] 23   91–98
- [ ] 24   99–104
- [ ] 25   105–107
- [ ] 26   108–113
- [ ] 27   114–118
- [ ] 28   119
- [ ] 29   120–134
- [ ] 30   135–142

July

❑	1	143–150

Proverbs

❑	2	1–3
❑	3	4–7
❑	4	8–11
❑	5	12–15
❑	6	16–18
❑	7	19–21
❑	8	22–24
❑	9	25–28
❑	10	29–31

Ecclesiastes

❑	11	1–4
❑	12	5–8
❑	13	9–12

Song of Solomon

❑	14	1–4
❑	15	5–8

Isaiah

❑	16	1–4
❑	17	5–8
❑	18	9–12
❑	19	13–15
❑	20	16–20
❑	21	21–24
❑	22	25–28
❑	23	29–32
❑	24	33–36
❑	25	37–40
❑	26	41–43
❑	27	44–46
❑	28	47–49
❑	29	50–52
❑	30	53–56
❑	31	57–60

August

❑	1	61–63
❑	2	64–66

Jeremiah

❑	3	1–3
❑	4	4–6
❑	5	7–9
❑	6	10–12
❑	7	13–15
❑	8	16–19
❑	9	20–22
❑	10	23–25
❑	11	26–29
❑	12	30–31
❑	13	32–34
❑	14	35–37
❑	15	38–40
❑	16	41–44
❑	17	45–48
❑	18	49–50
❑	19	51–52

Lamentations

❑	20	1–2
❑	21	3–5

Ezekiel

❑	22	1–4
❑	23	5–8
❑	24	9–12
❑	25	13–15
❑	26	16–17
❑	27	18–20
❑	28	21–23
❑	29	24–26
❑	30	27–29
❑	31	30–31

September

- ❑ 1   32–33
- ❑ 2   34–36
- ❑ 3   37–39
- ❑ 4   40–42
- ❑ 5   43–45
- ❑ 6   46–48

Daniel

- ❑ 7   1–2
- ❑ 8   3–4
- ❑ 9   5–6
- ❑ 10   7–9
- ❑ 11   10–12

Hosea

- ❑ 12   1–4
- ❑ 13   5–9
- ❑ 14   10–14
- ❑ 15   Joel

Amos

- ❑ 16   1–4
- ❑ 17   5–9
- ❑ 18   Obadiah and Jonah

Micah

- ❑ 19   1–4
- ❑ 20   5–7
- ❑ 21   Nahum
- ❑ 22   Habakkuk
- ❑ 23   Zephaniah
- ❑ 24   Haggai

Zechariah

- ❑ 25   1–4
- ❑ 26   5–9
- ❑ 27   10–14
- ❑ 28   Malachi

Matthew

❑	29	1–4
❑	30	5–7

October

❑	1	8–9
❑	2	10–11
❑	3	12–13
❑	4	14–16
❑	5	17–18
❑	6	19–20
❑	7	21–22
❑	8	23–24
❑	9	25–26
❑	10	27–28

Mark

❑	11	1–3
❑	12	4–5
❑	13	6–7
❑	14	8–9
❑	15	10–11
❑	16	12–13
❑	17	14
❑	18	15–16

Luke

❑	19	1–2
❑	20	3–4
❑	21	5–6
❑	22	7–8
❑	23	9–10
❑	24	11–12
❑	25	13–14
❑	26	15–16
❑	27	17–18
❑	28	19–20
❑	29	21–22
❑	30	23–24

John

❏	31	1–3

November

❏	1	4–5
❏	2	6–7
❏	3	8–9
❏	4	10–11
❏	5	12–13
❏	6	14–16
❏	7	17–19
❏	8	20–21

Acts

❏	9	1–3
❏	10	4–5
❏	11	6–7
❏	12	8–9
❏	13	10–11
❏	14	12–13
❏	15	14–15
❏	16	16–17
❏	17	18–19
❏	18	20–21
❏	19	22–23
❏	20	24–26
❏	21	27–28

Romans

❏	22	1–3
❏	23	4–6
❏	24	7–9
❏	25	10–12
❏	26	13–14
❏	27	15–16

1 Corinthians

❏	28	1–4
❏	29	5–7
❏	30	8–10

December

❏	1	11–13
❏	2	14–16

2 Corinthians

❏	3	1–4
❏	4	5–9
❏	5	10–13

Galatians

❏	6	1–3
❏	7	4–6

Ephesians

❏	8	1–3
❏	9	4–6
❏	10	**Philippians**
❏	11	**Colossians**
❏	12	**1 Thessalonians**
❏	13	**2 Thessalonians**
❏	14	**1 Timothy**
❏	15	**2 Timothy**
❏	16	**Titus and Philemon**

Hebrews

❏	17	1–4
❏	18	5–8
❏	19	9–10
❏	20	11–13
❏	21	**James**
❏	22	**1 Peter**
❏	23	**2 Peter**
❏	24	**1 John**
❏	25	**2, 3 John, Jude**

Revelation

❏	26	1–3
❏	27	4–8
❏	28	9–12
❏	29	13–16
❏	30	17–19
❏	31	20–22

Notes

1. Eleanor L. Doan, *The Speaker's Sourcebook* (Grand Rapids: Zondervan Publishing House, 1977), p. 96.
2. D.L. Moody, *Notes from My Bible* (Grand Rapids: Baker Book House, 1979), p. 199.
3. J. Oswald Sanders, *Spiritual Leadership* (Chicago: Moody Press, 1980), p. 123.
4. Terry Glaspey, *Pathway to the Heart of God* (Eugene, OR: Harvest House Publishers, 1998), p. 151.
5. Herbert Lockyer, *All the Promises of the Bible* (Grand Rapids, MI: Zondervan Publishing House, 1962), p. 10.
6. *Life Application Bible* (Wheaton, IL: Tyndale House Publishers, Inc. and Youth for Christ/USA 1988), p. 121.
7. Doan, *The Speaker's Sourcebook,* p. 176.
8. H. Dale Burke, *Less Is More Leadership* (Eugene, OR: Harvest House Publishers, 2004), p. 91.
9. R. Kent Hughes, *Disciplines of a Godly Man* (Wheaton, IL: Crossway Books, 1991), p. 62.
10. R. Kent Hughes, *Disciplines of a Godly Man,* p. 62.
11. *New Living Translation Bible* (Wheaton, IL: Tyndale House Publishers, Inc., 1996).
12. Adapted from Paul Little, *How to Give Away Your Faith* (Downers Grove, IL: InterVarsity Press, 1973), pp. 67-80.
13. J. Allan Petersen, *For Men Only,* quoting Pat Williams (Wheaton, IL: Tyndale House Publishers, 1974), p. 132. Pat Williams is the senior vice president of the NBA Orlando Magic, and this quote is used with permission.
14. Unknown source.
15. Unknown source.

Other Books by Jim George

A Young Man After God's Own Heart
Pursuing God really *is* an adventure—a lot like climbing a mountain. There are many challenges on the way up, but the great view at the top is well worth the trip. This book helps young men to experience the thrill of knowing real success in life—the kind that counts with God.

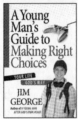

A Young Man's Guide to Making Right Choices
This book will help teen guys to think carefully about their decisions, assuring they gain the skills needed to face life's challenges.

A Young Man's Guide to Discovering His Bible
God's Word can change your life—for real. But that can't happen until you commit yourself to knowing the Bible. That's what this book by bestselling author Jim George is all about—knowing your Bible, discovering what it says, and making it your personal guide. You' II be surprised how relevant the Bible is in everything you do!

The Bare Bones Bible® Handbook for Teens
Based on the bestselling *Bare Bones Bible® Handbook*, this edition includes content and life applications specially written with teens in mind. You will be amazed at how much the Bible has to say about the things that matter most to you.

A Man After God's Own Heart

Many Christian men want to be men after God's own heart. …but how do they do this? George shows that a heartfelt desire to practice God's priorities is all that's needed. God's grace does the rest.

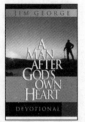

A Man After God's Own Heart Devotional

This book is filled with quick, focused devotions that will encourage your spiritual growth, equip you to persevere when life gets tough, manage your responsibilities well with wisdom, and live with maximum impact in all you do.

A Husband After God's Own Heart

You'll find your marriage growing richer and deeper as you pursue God and discover 12 areas in which you can make a real difference in your relationship with your wife.

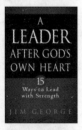

A Leader After God's Own Heart

Every man is either a leader or a leader in the making—whether at work, in the home, or any other setting. So what does it take to be a good leader—one God can use? This book will equip you to lead with strength and have a positive, lasting impact.

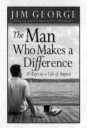

The Man Who Makes a Difference

How can you have a lasting impact? Here are the secrets to having a positive and meaningful influence in the lives of everyone you meet, including your wife and children.

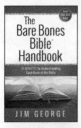

Bare Bones Bible® Handbook
The perfect resource for a fast and friendly overview of every book of the Bible. Excellent for anyone who wants to know the Bible better and get more from their interaction with God's Word.

10 Minutes to Knowing the Men and Women of the Bible
The lessons you can learn from the outstanding men and women of the Bible are powerfully relevant for today. As you review their lives, you'll discover special qualities worth emulating and life lessons for everyday living.

Know Your Bible from A to Z
This is a concise, easy-to-understand A-to-Z survey of the Bible's most important people, places, customs, and events. A great help for understanding the big picture of the Bible and applying the Scriptures to your daily life.

A Boy After God's Own Heart
This book helps boys learn how to make good decisions and great friends, see the benefits of homework and chores, get along better with their parents and siblings, and get into the Bible and grow closer to God.

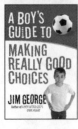

A Boy's Guide to Making Really Good Choices
Making good choices is the biggest step a boy can take toward growing up. This book helps boys learn to make the best kinds of choices—those that make them stronger, wiser, and more mature.

A Boy's Guide to Discovering His Bible
One of the most important things any child can do is to read the Bible daily. God has a lot to share, no matter what your age. Get to know your Bible better—it's an amazing adventure!

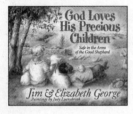

God Loves His Precious Children (coauthored with Elizabeth George)
Jim and Elizabeth George share the comfort and assurance of Psalm 23 with young children. Engaging watercolor scenes by artist Judy Luenebrink and delightful rhymes by Jim and Elizabeth bring the truths of each verse to life.

God's Wisdom for Little Boys (coauthored with Elizabeth George)
The wonderful teachings of Proverbs come to life for boys. Memorable rhymes play alongside colorful paintings for a charming presentation of truths to live by.

About the Author

Jim George is a bestselling author of more than a dozen books and a Bible teacher and Christian speaker. Two of his books were finalists for the Gold Medallion Book Award, *A Husband After God's Own Heart* and *A Young Man After God's Own Heart*.

Jim is the author of *A Young Man's Guide to Making Right Choices*. He has also written *The Bare Bones Bible® Handbook for Teens* and *A Young Man's Guide to Discovering His Bible,* both designed to help readers better understand their Bibles.

Jim holds Master of Divinity and Master of Theology degrees from Talbot School of Theology, and is married to Elizabeth George, also a bestselling Christian author. For information about Jim's speaking ministry, to sign up for his mailings, or to purchase his books, visit his website at:

www.JimGeorge.com

To learn more about Harvest House books and
to read sample chapters, visit our website:

www.harvesthousepublishers.com

HARVEST HOUSE PUBLISHERS
EUGENE, OREGON